Chris and Jim provide a systematic approach for cultivating generosity in your church and helping people understand that generosity is not something that God *wants from* you but is something God *has for* you. Read and apply what is in this book and you will lead a more generous church.
Dave Ferguson, lead pastor, Community Christian Church

I firmly believe that the key to winning with money is holding it with an open hand. In *Contagious Generosity*, Jim and Chris show you a better way to approach giving: God's way.
Dave Ramsey, New York Times *bestselling author*

Moving Christ followers to higher levels of generosity is challenging. Chris and Jim have leveraged years of observations into a highly practical book to encourage and equip leaders to overcome this challenge.
Brad Lomenick, executive director, Catalyst

I've seen the limitations the lack of generosity places on mission and ministry. In *Contagious Generosity*, Chris and Jim take on the topic with boldness and wisdom. Get a team of your leaders to read this book with you and then start implementing the ideas in your church.
Ed Stetzer, www.edstetzer.com

The generosity conversation is crucial to discipleship and to funding the mission of the church. All too often, the church avoids the topic and pays a big price for it. I am grateful to Chris and Jim for taking the topic head-on with practical advice based on their hands-on experience with so many churches!
Howard Dayton, founder, Compass—finances God's way

Pastors make two major mistakes with regard to money. They either talk about money too little, or they talk about it apart from whole-life discipleship. Chris and Jim challenge our assumptions and plot a compelling course for those who lead the church.
Darrin Patrick, lead pastor, The Journey,
St. Louis; author, For the City

It will change the way your church views money, giving, and the power of radical generosity.
Greg Surratt, lead pastor, Seacoast Church; author, Ir-Rev-Rend

Chris and Jim, out of their work with hundreds of churches, have made some keen observations that will help any church become more strategic with the generosity conversation. Be prepared to be challenged and equipped!

Tony Morgan, author, coach, consultant, TonyMorganLive.com

This book will help you and your church create a genuine long-term culture of generosity. I encourage you to read it!

Larry Osborne, author and pastor,
North Coast Church, Vista, California

Contagious Generosity is a perfect practical resource to help us cultivate a culture of giving in our churches. Chris and Jim have included biblical how-to's for you to implement in the life of your church to increase the DNA of generosity.

Dino Rizzo, lead pastor, Healing Place Church; author, Servolution

This book will challenge you but not leave you wondering what to do. Grab something to take notes with and let Jim and Chris disciple you to create a culture of generosity in your church.

Gunnar Johnson, executive pastor,
financial stewardship, Gateway Church

The generosity conversation is being overlooked by too many pastors and church leaders. We have to grow ourselves and our people in the area. Contagious Generosity has opened the door for church leaders to help build a culture of generosity.

Jamie Munson, author, Money: God or Gift?

As Jim's pastor, I have seen firsthand the effect of his generosity conversations at Perimeter Church. I am glad to see he has partnered with Chris Willard to put their collective thoughts in writing and get this message out. This topic is relevant and necessary in the church today.

Randy Pope, senior pastor, Perimeter Church

Chris and Jim provide a practical look at raising the tide of generosity in the local church. A must-read for any leader who is serious about taking their church on the generosity journey.

Scott Ridout, lead pastor,
Sun Valley Community Church

Chris and Jim have a solid understanding of how to build a culture of generosity in the church. *Contagious Generosity* is a guide for church leaders who want to impact their church culture and thereby impact the world.

Chris Goulard, pastor of stewardship
and benevolence ministries, Saddleback Church

An incredibly valuable resource for anyone interested in helping others get infected by a contagious generosity.

Dick Towner, executive director, Good $ense Movement

Get the book, circle up with your leaders, and get a movement of contagious generosity started in your church!

Toby Slough, lead pastor, Cross Timbers Community Church

Jim and Chris are two of the wisest mentors in the world when it comes to developing a culture of generosity. This work is not simply about increasing our giving. It's about God's heart being expressed in people's hearts and lives. Every pastor in America should read this book, then apply it to their own lives.

Shawn Lovejoy, pastor, Mountain Lake Church

Read *Contagious Generosity* for its dozens of uplifting stories, insights, and practical tools to get your team moving forward in this vital area.

Dave Travis, chief executive officer and
chief encouragement officer, Leadership Network

Having been a senior pastor, I know firsthand the importance of raising generous people in the local church. Now as i work with churches across the country on staffing issues, I see it even more. *Contagious Generosity* is an excellent road map to developing the giving gifts of your people

William Vanderbloemen, president,
The Vanderbloemen Search Group

As a pastor who struggles with "talking about money," I found this book to be a most valuable resource for my ministry. It is not about money; it is about changing lives and hearts.

Dr. Joel C. Hunter, senior pastor, Northland—
A Church Distributed, Longwood, Florida

Contagious Generosity will be on my required reading list for all my church clients.

Jim Tomberlin, founder and chief strategist,
MultiSite Solutions

Contagious Generosity is a compelling and practical call to church and lay leaders to cultivate a culture of generosity as an expression of God's transforming power in the life of Christ followers.

Todd Harper, president, Generous Giving

Chock-full of 24-karat insight, this book is an unmatched collection of gold, mined and refined by two of the best guides on the planet.

Will Mancini, founder, Auxano; author, Church Unique

This book is worth reading with all your leaders. Chris and Jim take us beyond tactics, beyond strategy, to the deeper issue of culture, which when nurtured can flourish into radical generosity that brings joy to people and honor to God.

Bruce B. Miller, senior pastor, Christ Fellowship; author,
The Leadership Baton

Chris and Jim provide pastors and church leaders with a workable strategy to release the potential of generosity for the work of God's kingdom in the world around us. Buy this book and keep it close!

Mike Glenn, senior pastor,
Brentwood Baptist, Brentwood, Tennessee

When pastors ask me questions about generosity and church finances, I refer them to Jim Sheppard. Now we have the book!

Dick Kaufmann, senior pastor,
Harbor Presbyterian Church, San Diego

Contagious Generosity holds both practical and strategic insights for church leaders to ignite a viral spirit of giving among Christ followers. Embracing this book will free the church to mobilize disciples for ministry.

Sharla Bickley Langston, director, Generous Community
Development for the National Christian Foundation of North Texas

CONTAGIOUS
GENEROSITY

The Leadership Network Innovation Series

Leadership Network
Innovation Series

CONTAGIOUS GENEROSITY

Creating a Culture of Giving in Your Church

CHRIS WILLARD & JIM SHEPPARD

Foreword by Robert Morris

ZONDERVAN®

ZONDERVAN.com/
AUTHORTRACKER
follow your favorite authors

We want to hear from you. Please send your comments about this book to us in care of zreview@zondervan.com. Thank you.

ZONDERVAN

Contagious Generosity
Copyright © 2012 by Chris Willard and James E. Sheppard

This title is also available as a Zondervan ebook.

Requests for information should be addressed to:

Zondervan, *Grand Rapids, Michigan 49530*

Library of Congress Cataloging-in-Publication Data

Willard, Chris, 1964–
    Contagious generosity : creating a culture of giving in your church / Chris Willard and Jim Sheppard.
      p. cm.
    ISBN 978-0-310-89313-4 (softcover)
    1. Generosity—Religious aspects—Christianity. 2. Christian giving. 3. Christian stewardship. I. Sheppard, Jim, 1954- II. Title.
BV4647.G45W55 2012
248'.6—dc23
                                  2012005298

Cover design: Christopher Tobias
Cover photography: Haag + Kropp GbR / artpartner-images.com
Interior design: Matthew VanZomeren

Printed in the United States of America

12 13 14 15 16 17 18 /DCI/ 20 19 18 17 16 15 14 13 12 11 10 9 8 7 6 5 4 3 2 1

To my mom and dad, who lived generously and modeled uncon-
ditional love for me. To my girls, Anna and Emily — there was
a time when we thought we would not be able to have kids, but
God knew different, and he gave you to us. You are the mani-
festation of his generous grace in our lives. And most of all to
Nancy, who said "I do" many years ago. You have been generous
with your love for me and your forgiveness of me, and it has
changed the way I live.   — *Jim Sheppard*

To my children, CJ, Hannah, and Natalie, I am so proud of
you and thankful for all you have taught me about what really
matters. And, most of all, to my wife, the fabulous Susan. What
would I do without you? I am so thankful for everything you
have done that has helped me become the man I am today.
                                                  — *Chris Willard*

CONTENTS

PART 1 CHURCH DEVELOPMENT

Culture represents the "permission system" which is unique to each church. Culture is either a headwind or a tailwind to creating a culture of generosity. Generosity should not be a silo. It should be a thread that runs through the organization and mission of the entire church.

A church must have a strategy to lead its people to become generous. It is more than just "want to"; it must include "how to." Good strategy is both informational and transformational. Lasting change requires both dimensions.

Generosity begets generosity. People instinctively know whether a church is generous. There is a viral effect of generosity on others.

PART 2 LEADERSHIP DEVELOPMENT

Generous churches are led by generous leaders. A generous pastor can lead a church that is not generous, but a generous church doesn't exist apart from a generous leader.

FOREWORD

When I wrote *The Blessed Life*, it was my hope that Christians everywhere would be inspired to live a life of generosity. Generosity and giving are incredibly important to me. As I've followed God's principles of giving, there are many times I have found myself on the giving and receiving ends of generosity. I've experienced the "blessed life" that results from obeying God in this area, and I find it so important to communicate this truth to others that it has become my life message.

As Gateway Church has grown over the last twelve years, the Lord has directed us to make generosity a core value of everything we do. We know God has called us to wisely manage our finances, as a church and as individuals, so we can be the people he has called us to be. I want my congregation to be financially healthy so they can enthusiastically participate in God's work in the kingdom.

That being said, I want to emphasize that we do not pursue generosity and stewardship as a fundraising strategy for our church. Our main goal is to raise up generous stewards. The point is to *give*, not to get. When you understand that everything you have comes from God, you'll have no problem using your resources to build his kingdom. He will take care of the rest.

Over the years, I've met many pastors who have asked me for help in this area. There are many churches that spend too much time focusing on making the budget work for their needs, not for the needs of the kingdom. Their hearts are in the right place, but they need practical ways to grow generosity in their hearts and in the hearts of their congregation.

I am thankful that Jim Sheppard and Chris Willard have collaborated to bring their shared observations to the church. Their advice, which is the result of countless hours with hundreds of churches, is not to be ignored. I loved the chapter "Follow Me," in which they show how generosity has to start with leadership. I know that in order for Gateway to be a generous church, I first have to be a generous leader. The Lord has helped my wife, Debbie, and me to be generous leaders, a standard which is now mirrored in our church. Because of this generosity, God has done and is doing incredible things through Gateway Church.

I know the Lord wants to work the miracle of generosity in your church too. *Contagious Generosity* will transform your thinking on biblical stewardship. Take these principles to heart as you seek to encourage and grow the people the Lord has placed under your care.

—*Robert Morris, pastor, Gateway Church*

INTRODUCTION
WHAT IS GENEROSITY?

> You will be enriched in every way so that you can be gener-
> ous on every occasion, and through us your generosity will
> result in thanksgiving to God.   —*2 Corinthians 9:11*

Within the church, there is currently a significant "generosity movement," but generosity is also a debated topic among Christian leaders. How we understand the role of generosity in our lives—and in the Christian communities in which we do life together—perhaps says more about our faith and our understanding of the gospel than any other single aspect of our faith.

Christian leaders tend to fall into one of three categories. Those in the first category have adopted generosity as the standard by which they live out their faith. It is the lens through which they interpret the will of God and their role in his kingdom on earth. Those in the second category embrace generosity as an appropriate substitute for the more established language of stewardship. For decades, the language of stewardship has been used to refer to believers' responsibility to support the work of the church and to faithfully use their resources to serve its mission. Finally, those in the third category are skeptical of the notion of generosity. This group includes Christian leaders who are disillusioned by the church and its relationship with money. They see hypocrisy and sense that there is a fundamental disconnection between what the church practices and the biblical principles of stewardship that the church teaches.

These three groups view the same subject — how our faith informs our relationship to money — through three perpectives. But they have more in common than they might think.

We believe it is necessary to view generosity through each perspective and to learn where these views converge based on what the Bible teaches. Doing so will lead to a shift in lifestyle among the followers of Christ — nothing short of a revolution, one that will attract countless people who are looking for a new way to live that is not based on self-serving motives but instead represents the heart of the one who made us and generously gave himself for us.

A Working Definition

Let's begin with a working definition of generosity. Generosity is at its core a lifestyle, a lifestyle in which we share all that we have, are, and ever will become as a demonstration of God's love and a response to God's grace. It is not enough for the church to talk about generosity, nor is it enough for individual Christians simply to commit to being generous. What makes generosity a real and powerful witness to God's love is our action. Generosity flows from an understanding that all that we have, are, and ever will become is not ours to possess, and it results in sharing what we've been given with others for the advancement of the kingdom and the glory of God. Generosity embraces a biblical understanding of stewardship:

- God is the owner of everything.
- What we have has been given to us by God.
- The resources we possess are assets to be invested in the kingdom.

Before we can be generous, we must understand what it means to be a steward, recognizing that what we have is not ours to own and confessing that Jesus is Lord over our money, possessions, positions of authority, and talents. You can't be generous without the discipline of biblical stewardship, and biblical stewardship demands generosity. The gift of God's grace shapes our faith and leads to the conviction that all that we have—our time, talent, treasure, and testimony—has been given to us for a purpose. We cannot separate our acceptance of God's grace from the practice of generosity. We are generous because God was first generous to us, freely giving his life for our sakes. As followers of Christ, we seek to imitate the one who gave himself for us (1 Thess. 1:6; 2:14). Stewardship is more than an obligation. It's an opportunity to witness to the reckless nature of the God who gives the gift of salvation by grace to all who will receive it. Generosity is the fullest expression of the life of a steward, one who has been given a gift that must be used wisely and for a purpose, bringing glory to God.

Why Should I Care?

Given the challenges that many individuals, families, and churches are facing in the aftermath of the global economic crisis that began in late 2008, the topic of this book is more timely now than ever before. When our security is threatened by job loss or scarcity, we are tempted to lock up what we've stored away. But God is working in amazing ways as churches and individuals choose the opposite approach. Instead of fearfully locking away their resources, they choose to share what they have with people in need, and their generous giving has drawn attention. In some cases, these faith communities received local and national media coverage for their acts of generosity. Even though their financial security was uncertain, some churches gave away their surplus to meet the desperate needs of people in their communities. This act of generosity, motivated by love for God, earned these churches credibility and made an impact on their communities, changing the lives of those who gave as well as of those who received. The financial crisis became a bridge that enabled the church to take the message of a generous God to a struggling world. Churches, in ways they never had done before, began to talk about money, teaching their people how to gain freedom from debt and emphasizing the discipline of sacrificial giving.

Generosity, when it flows naturally from the heart of a church community, is contagious. It has an undeniable effect on people who come into contact with it. It expresses in practical and powerful ways the message at the core of our faith: God gave his only Son to us that we might have life. Generous churches believe that they have been given everything, and as an expression of their love for God, they share what they have with one another and with people in need.

Who This Book Is For (and Who It's Not For)

This book is based on our individual experiences and observations over nearly twenty years as we have worked with hundreds of churches, consulting and teaching on the topic of stewardship and generosity. Most recently it was born of a multiyear emphasis, organized by Leadership Network, called the Generous Church Leadership Community. Church staffs from across the country came together to talk about the ways in which generosity was changing their church communities. Leaders listened to each other, sharing what worked, what didn't, and what they had learned along the way.

We wrote this book to speak to the concerns of those who are leading churches and missional communities and who are working to maximize kingdom impact through local church ministry. We appreciate these leaders' dedication and obedience to God's call, and we sincerely hope this book will encourage you and challenge you. This is not an academic text, nor is it a theological book. Neither of us are qualified to address the subject of generosity in those ways. However, we acknowledge that this book has significant theological implications. Our intent is to facilitate a much broader conversation about generosity, based on the experience of church leaders and our own experience as guides to church leaders on this topic.

We also wrote this book for individual believers. Some of the greatest movements in history began because individuals didn't wait for those in positions of leadership to take the first step. Perhaps you want more from your faith experience but just aren't sure what that looks like. You are curious about generosity, and your desire is to practice generosity in your personal life and inspire it in the life of your church. In an attempt to make this book as valuable as possible, we decided to limit its scope by addressing two things: financial generosity and how our generosity relates to the church. We acknowledge that there are many books that address generosity and that there are often many generous individuals within a church. But this book is intended to focus on those aspects of generosity that apply to the corporate experience of the church.

The local church is the primary means that God uses to build his kingdom on earth. And every local church has a unique culture that shapes its identity. Our personal beliefs are grounded in our culture. Our actions reflect our culture. And our impact on our community is determined largely by our culture. We believe that church leaders have been given the primary responsibility for creating a culture of faith and practice that aligns with biblical teaching on generosity.

We also limited our conversation about generosity to money and finances. We certainly believe that generosity can be expressed in many other ways, but one of the most common ways in which people give to the work of the church is through financial gifts, so we've limited our focus in order to make this book a valuable tool for church leaders.

Money is perhaps the most measurable aspect of our faith. How we spend our money reflects our commitment to our faith, indicating whether we practice what we say we believe. But that same standard also should be applied to our churches, corporately. How a church uses the resources God has entrusted to it is a reflection of what the church values and what it believes. A church that does not reflect a generous spirit will struggle to grow and disciple generous givers.

Two Guides

Imagine sitting in a tree by a river, watching boats dock and unload their cargo. If you spent enough time in that tree, you would observe some patterns. Some of the boats' crews would work more effectively, while others would make decisions that lead to mishaps. After watching long enough, you might anticipate the success of the docking process, based on the initial moves made by the boat and its crew.

We didn't write this book because we are more gifted or more qualified than you are to lead your church. Instead this book synthesizes our observations of countless churches as they navigate the challenges of developing a culture of generosity. After watching long enough, we've learned to anticipate what is likely to happen when a church takes specific steps.

Chris Willard has served in several strategic roles within parachurch ministry, on executive church staff, and now as director of generosity initiatives for Leadership Network. Part of his role is to organize leaders around strategic subjects, like generosity, and help them to dig deep in order to gain a broader, deeper understanding of a particular subject's application in local church ministry. The other part of his role is to work one-on-one with churches to help them implement thoughts, ideas, and practices that are proven to accelerate generosity.

Jim Sheppard began his career in the world of accounting and finance. Working with numbers is a natural gifting for Jim that God later used in a way Jim never anticipated. As a principal of

Generis, an innovative church-generosity consulting firm, Jim, like Chris, works with churches to help them navigate the waters of everyday giving, project giving, and legacy giving.

Together we have worked with leaders in the Christian community to answer their questions, advise their decision making, and help them inspire a spirit of contagious generosity that transforms their churches from institutions that protect a tradition to communities of faith that engage in changing lives. We know that many pastors sit on the edges of this conversation. They want to know more, do more, and be more radical in their generosity. Some are simply waiting for an invitation. Consider yourself invited, and prepare to join a movement that is sweeping Christian communities around the world.

There is no list of ten steps to success hidden within the pages of this book. Instead we invite you to grow, to learn, and to struggle through the complex issues every church deals with:

- What is generosity?
- What does being a generous church look like?
- How can I encourage the members of my church to be more generous?
- What is God calling us to do that we never dreamt would be possible?
- Who can benefit from our financial blessing?
- How can we use our excess to transform the communities where we live and work and play?
- What can we do to free people from unbiblical habits related to money?
- What does leading my church to be generous mean for me as pastor or leader?

There is no quick fix, fast track, or answer key in this book. Leading your church to become a generous church often begins with an honest appraisal and a time of confession, bringing your personal habits with money into the light of God's truth. You may need to repair some relationships with your church leadership, depending on how you've made financial decisions in the past. Perhaps you'll also need to make some adjustments by adding or removing positions in your staff and organizational structure. The changes God is calling you to make will not be easy. There is a cost to everything we do. Jesus warned people who were interested in following him that they had to be willing to put aside their own desires, leaving what was comfortable and accepting the cost. They had to put their feet into action and follow him. The same is true for us. If we want to be churches that create a culture of reckless, contagious generosity, we need to be willing to pay the price.

The Decision Is Yours

The Old Testament book of 1 Kings relates a story of a widow and her son, a family so impoverished that they have enough flour and oil left for only one more meal. They are prepared to eat their final meal and then die. The prophet Elijah is in town that day, visiting the drought-stricken region, and he asks this poor woman for some bread and water. At first the woman assures the prophet that she does not have enough food to feed all three of them, but he tells her first to make him a loaf of bread and then to bake one for herself and her son. He encourages her, telling her not to be afraid and promising her that God will not let the oil or the flour run out before the drought is over.

In faith, the widow obeys the word of the prophet and finds that she does indeed have enough flour and oil to feed them all. Not only that, but both her flour jar and her oil jug remain full until the rains return and the drought ends. She and her son are kept alive, demonstrating the abundant life that God is ready to give us when we choose to step out in faith and share what he has given to us.

This pattern of faith-filled, sacrificial generosity is in direct conflict with a theme in American culture. We Americans perpetuate the myth that tells us that we must be independent, providing for ourselves, and that we must pull ourselves up by our own bootstraps. We believe that we are responsible for our own success and therefore that whatever success we find is ours to keep and to use to meet our desires and needs. But as followers of Christ, we have a different perspective. We understand that everything we have is not just something we've earned or deserve; it's a gift of God's grace. We recognize that we are stewards and that everything we have belongs to God and is intended to be invested in the growth of the kingdom. Developing a culture of generosity begins with an understanding of who owns what. If I own what I have, am, and will become, then it is mine to give at my discretion. But if God owns it all, then I am merely an instrument of generosity designed to distribute his resources for the abundant advancement of the kingdom.

Unfortunately, much of American Christianity has tended to believe that we have to preserve our wealth in order to meet our own needs and that being generous is a matter of convenience. In their book *Passing the Plate* (Oxford, 2008), Christian Smith and Michael Emerson introduce the phrase "discretionary obligation" as a way to understand the typical American Christian's approach to giving. Smith and Emerson suggest that Christians believe that they should give generously to the kingdom, yet at the same time feel free to give at their discretion, giving only what they can, when they can, and never feeling burdened by a compulsion to give. If "discretionary obligation" defines our understanding of generosity, we will never experience true abundance in our churches.

Though many Americans have faced significant financial setbacks in recent years, we have observed that wealth in America has increased at a record pace over the last sixty years, even after taking into account the economic retraction of 2008. However, the percentage of income Americans give to churches has been decreasing over the same period of time. This just doesn't make sense. We have more than ever, but we give less than ever. The American church can no longer turn its back on this issue. It is time to take a look at ways we can reverse this disturbing trend of more wealth and less giving to the church.

The culture of a church is revealed when there is a crisis of faith. When the global recession hit in 2008, some churches thrived, some churches plateaued, and some churches declined. Few churches had a safety net, so a portion of those that declined did so with great speed. Some churches responded in fear, locking up whatever cash they had in order to weather the storm. Others decided to take another path, recognizing that the recession had revealed significant need in their communities.

In our conversations with church leaders, we found that many of the churches that chose to share, even when there wasn't a clear path to replenishment, experienced something unexpected and transformational: abundance, learning that there were more resources available to them than they had ever imagined. They used what God had given them to prevent foreclosures, promote adoptions of orphans, feed the hungry, help those living in extreme poverty, and assist communities recovering from natural disasters. These churches witnessed a level of spiritual formation that rapidly and holistically changed their cultures.

We had a front-row seat as a number of these churches processed what they were experiencing as individuals and corporately. We have worked hard to harness the observations we've made along the way. But if all you do is read this book, then we have not done our jobs. Our hopes and prayers are grounded in the expectation that you will become more intentional about building a culture of generosity in your church so that your church can be an accurate reflection of the Christ we profess as Lord and Savior.

CHURCH
DEVELOPMENT

Chapter 1

CULTURE IS KEY

> Give, and it will be given to you. A good measure, pressed down, shaken together and running over, will be poured into your lap. For with the measure you use, it will be measured to you. —*Luke 6:38*

In many ways, a church is like a family. In most families, it is just understood who sits at the head of the table at Thanksgiving dinner, who cuts the turkey, and how the food will be passed around. As churches grow, they become less like a nuclear family and more like a family reunion. You know that you're related to each other, but you don't know everyone's name or all the family rules. And, accidentally, you may sit in Uncle Harry's seat and unintentionally create a memorable holiday experience.

A church must be intentional about developing a culture of generosity from the outset, because the culture of the church is the most powerful way of effecting corporate change. If a church isn't clear about what it believes on the topic of giving and stewardship, then its members won't be either. The culture of a church includes its customs and its underlying attitudes. It answers the question, How do we get things done around here? First-time visitors intuitively sense the culture, and even outsiders can describe

it to others. Culture sets the tone, defines the pace, and becomes the catalyst for vision, strategy, goals, and impact.

The staff at Sun Valley Community Church near Phoenix, Arizona, understands the need to be clear about their commitment to generosity. Lead teaching pastor Chad Moore, lead pastor Scott Ridout, and the rest of the founding staff have communicated their conviction to be generous since the inception of the church. Chad describes it like this: "From the very beginning, there was an intentionality about placing stewardship, giving, and generosity at the forefront of who we are." Chad describes it as a combination of teaching, action, and expectation. "There was no way someone could be part of Sun Valley for very long and not *get* generosity.... This is not about a curriculum. It's all about transformation of the heart." The leaders at Sun Valley Church have sought to establish a process that encourages transformation, not just another program to help people meet a felt need. They have sought to develop a culture that invites people to change their hearts, minds, and habits—especially when it comes to generosity.

Many churches start addressing the topic of generosity with a program or a class on dealing with debt. While we would agree that debt is a huge problem that needs to be addressed, debt is merely a symptom of a much larger heart issue. A person struggling with debt needs more than a few helpful suggestions or good financial advice. They must learn what it means to be a generous Christian, a person who looks at the world through a different lens. A generous Christian is grounded in a certain view of that world that enables them to give freely to others in an authentic, genuine way. And the same is true for generous churches. Most people outside of the church likely would not consider generosity to be a defining characteristic of a faith community. Instead they would expect rules, obligations, and expectations that define and shape the culture of a church. This is why even critics and skeptics are caught off guard when they encounter a church culture in which people freely share what they have for the advancement of the kingdom.

Leaders often underestimate the role that culture plays in shaping the habits of a community of believers. Many believers have been taught that giving is a private matter, an individual experience, something that is just between them and God. Some church cultures even discourage people from talking about financial matters. Yet by counting the number of verses in Scripture, you could argue that Jesus spent more time talking about money and possessions than about any other subject, including heaven and hell. Why? Because Jesus knew that how we handle our money is more than a private matter. A heart of generosity is shaped by the culture of our church. In other words, that culture directly shapes and influences our spiritual transformation.

If you want to see lasting transformation in your church, it begins with the culture. Culture is not neutral. If the culture is not right, it will be a headwind resisting almost everything you try to do. If the culture is right, it will be a tailwind accelerating everything you try to do.

Why Is Culture Important?

Knowing the culture of a community can allow you to predict how its people will respond in a given situation. When the U.S. economy took a nosedive in 2008, churches reacted in wildly different ways, depending on their attitudes, beliefs, and practices. In general, we saw churches respond in one of three ways: denial, survival, or advancement.

Some churches denied that anything was happening. Like a child who covers his eyes and thinks he is invisible, some church leaders decided behind closed doors that if they didn't talk about the loss of giving and financial support, then it wasn't real. Churches that denied that the recession was happening created confusion for the people in the pew. Why? Because the people in the congregation were talking about the reality of what they were experiencing, often with little input from their spiritual leaders.

Other churches decided that their goal was survival. Leaders locked down on ministry budgets, temporarily or permanently stopped investing in any "nonessential" ministry, and put on hold any plans for growth or expansion. Unfortunately, many of the people in their churches followed suit, tightening their giving and holding back on any nonessential gifts. While the leaders' decisions may have seemed prudent, in the long run they simply revealed the leaders' deeper priorities. Only the ministries deemed worthy of funding were kept and supported.

Finally, some church leaders decided to accept the reality of the economy, face it head-on, and unleash all that God had entrusted to them, knowing that adversity can create opportunities to present people with the gospel. We watched in awe as we saw church leaders giving freely from their rainy-day funds. They sacrificially and without producing a deficit built their annual operational budgets on fifty or fifty-one weeks' worth of offerings instead of fifty-two so that they could give away the surplus. And they repositioned their ministries to meet the physical, mental, and spiritual needs of people who were experiencing significant trauma because of the financial crisis. Churches that responded in this way saw a similar response among their members. In the midst of financial challenges, people sold their cars, postponed vacations, and decided not to buy that bigger, better home, all in an effort to help others. It is no accident that leaders who opted to be generous when they could have justified playing it safe created a catalytic response within their congregations.

One of the greatest responsibilities churches have is the spiritual formation of their members — moving people from where they are today toward living in a way that is more consistent with the picture of the Jesus we see in the Gospels. The culture of a church plays a significant role in determining how well individual followers of Christ represent him. Culture constantly takes on new forms within a congregation. It is dynamic, representing the sum of the beliefs, attitudes, and behaviors of the people. But the mix of people in a church is constantly changing as new members join and other members move away. Because of this dynamism, a church leader who wants to create a culture of generosity in his church will need to develop a systematic process of spiritual formation. There is no status quo in a church culture; a church is either moving toward or moving away from becoming a generous church. Either you are leading your people toward a lifestyle of biblical generosity, or you are watching them drift toward selfishness and the world's economy. A generous church culture must be constantly, intentionally influenced until it results in the contagious generosity of the congregation.

Culture Trumps Vision

Church leaders often talk about the vision of the church. Any successful organization — for-profit or nonprofit — knows that it must define a clear and compelling vision in order to move forward. And churches too need a vision that can be clearly articulated and translated into measurable results. But having the right vision for generosity isn't enough.

Vision describes a picture of the desired future of the church. And the culture of the church defines the path and possibility of realizing that vision. Even well-executed tactics will fail unless they are grounded in the specific context and culture of the church community. In other words, it's not enough to say that we want to be a generous church. We must also ensure that the steps we take toward generosity are natural, taken in a way that fits the church's culture, rather than contrived. If we seek change from people but fail to develop a culture that inspires and supports generous habits, we should not expect to achieve the long-term vision of having a more generous church.

Beliefs determine actions. This is why it is essential to look deep into the culture of your church, to look closely at what you do and say that is shaping the beliefs, thoughts, and actions of your members. This is where so many leaders miss the opportunity for transformation. They wrongly assume that including the theme of generosity in their vision or preaching on generosity once a year will magically create generous people in their congregations. They lack a plan to create a culture of generosity, and the vision goes no farther than a closed-door, staff meeting conversation. Instead culture must be shaped by intentional, systematic processes.

A system is a process by which an intended result is produced, manufactured, or created. There are specific steps in the process, and a clear goal or outcome is carefully defined. Systems engineers spend their lives creating these types of systems in manufacturing environments, and while you may not have a church staff position with that title, it's necessary to think through your church culture in this type of systematic manner if you wish to achieve the result: a culture in which generosity is contagious.

We like to call this "cultivating the culture." Cultivate is a word laden with meaning. To cultivate something involves working it to develop it and to help it grow. When farmers cultivate crops, they prepare the soil, plant the seeds, water, weed, fertilize, and finally harvest. It's difficult, labor-intensive work that requires patience, attention, and skill. The cultivation process isn't quick—crops don't grow overnight—and it's not advisable to try to speed it up or skip a step, since every part of it is integral to the whole. Every aspect of the process builds momentum and works with the others to yield a harvest that will feed and sustain people.

As human beings, we also cultivate, or develop, certain abilities over time. As we grow from babes into young children, we learn how to roll over, crawl, walk, run, and jump. We don't just wake up one day able to perform these functions. Growth comes after observing others, finding the will to try, attempting and failing, trying again with a little encouragement, and finally succeeding and moving on to the next milestone.

The process of developing a culture of generosity in your church is no different. This isn't something that just happens, and cultivating a culture like this doesn't just hinge on one thing—a silver bullet or magic key that solves all your problems. Having a clear vision and lots of energy and willpower will not make your church more generous. Generosity is a fruit of God's grace, the product of a transformed heart, and it develops in an atmosphere that encourages it, celebrates it, and reproduces it consistently over time.

Culture Finds Substance in Life Change

The culture of a church is most clearly evidenced by life change. Too often, church leaders are tempted to allow the management of time, programs, and budgets to detract from the ultimate goal of any Christian community: changed lives. Changed lives are the greatest evidence of the church's supernatural blessing. What are you seeing in your church? Are you seeing new Christians emerge from your community? Are you watching Christ followers make new commitments in their faith? Are you observing mature Christians growing in the application and discipline of their faith?

Those who wish to lead their churches to develop a culture of contagious generosity need to be clear from the very beginning that their goal is not to raise more money, to build bigger buildings, or to increase their budget. All of these things may happen, but they are simply the means by which people are transformed into the likeness of Christ. We see the fruit of contagious generosity not when budget numbers rise but when a college student sells her car and gives the proceeds to people in need, when a family decides not to take that expensive vacation and uses the money for a kingdom purpose, or when a senior adult reorients his financial goals so he can give away more of his money both today and after his death. These outward measurements of change are the evidence of generosity in a church and the signs that a spirit of generosity has integrated with the church's culture.

In the past, many churches looked to an annual stewardship sermon or an occasional capital funds appeal as a way of generating more giving. These types of events do have their place and can encourage a certain level of spiritual growth and development, but they tend to have a limited impact. They fail to effectively disciple people in the spiritual practice of generous giving and lack the power to foster a consistent spirit of generosity. Sometimes a simpler approach can lead to unexpected opportunities for God to work in people's hearts. A need can be presented, a request made, and people can simply be invited to give.

In some cases, a need can be so compelling that a congregation will respond almost immediately. Asbury United Methodist Church in Tulsa, Oklahoma, experienced this when its staff wanted to raise money to purchase Bibles for children in the persecuted church. The fit seemed perfect, since Asbury's DNA is built on a deep reverence for Scripture, an emphasis on children, and a heart for missions. Rather than assembling a committee, developing a new program, or launching a fundraising drive, the staff settled on a much simpler strategy. They dedicated just five minutes of one worship service to sharing the need. The straightforward pitch essentially asked two questions:

1. "Can you imagine what your life would be like if you didn't have a Bible?"
2. "Can you imagine how these children's lives would be enriched if they had Bibles?"

That simple message instantly resonated with the congregation. In five minutes, the congregation learned enough to know that their giving could make a real difference. The result? The offering produced special gifts totaling $25,000 for the persecuted church. That's a testament to both the church's generosity and the power of a compelling message. Leaders of generous churches like Asbury have learned that generosity is so much more than a program, a special emphasis, or a campaign. Generosity is the natural and appropriate response of people who have been confronted with the grace of God.

Culture Is Shaped by Values

We frequently see churches consign the topic of generosity to the realm of financial administration. As long as enough money is coming in, the pastor doesn't have to preach about giving or encourage a special offering. But we must not forget that culture is shaped by what we value. And when church leaders don't value generosity, it's unlikely that the people in the church will either.

In our interviews with hundreds of church staff members—from children's ministry leaders to senior adult leaders—we've found that when we begin asking questions about the topics of financial stewardship and generosity, confidence wanes and people have difficulty articulating what their church believes. Thankfully, a growing trend in churches, particularly generous churches, is to include words like *stewardship*, *generosity*, and *giving* as part of their core values. But what does this really look like?

Brian Tome, senior pastor of Crossroads Church in Cincinnati, Ohio, regrets not talking about money with his congregation sooner: "By not talking about God's perspective of money and possessions, we conditioned people to become consumers instead of givers." Brian believes that it's necessary to clearly communicate that the goal of giving is not just funding local church ministry; it's participating in a revolution that God is orchestrating through believers around the world.

That shift in thinking about the purpose of giving was instrumental in cultivating a culture of generosity at Crossroads. About five years ago Brian sat in the atrium of their new church building.

The church had doubled in attendance in three months, and that day God helped Brian to think clearly about the future of the church if it continued to grow. Brian realized that they would soon outgrow the building they'd just built, so they'd have to build a bigger facility, and then a larger one, and later a still larger one. "It looked like an endless treadmill," he remembers. Instead of simply thinking about bigger buildings, he and his leadership team met to develop a larger vision, one with a focus on the kingdom instead of merely the future of their church. "We realized we're not just here to fund our local church ministry," Brian relates. "We're part of a revolution God initiated to change the world. That revolution starts with every person at our church being a blessing to people around them — and eventually being a blessing to people around the world. That's what God promised Abraham in Genesis 12."

The church now operates with three guiding principles when they plan and talk about their financial future.

1. Bless people.
2. Base the budget on what we believe God wants, not on what we think we'll get.
3. Spend it; don't save it.

People in the church give because they know that the money will be spent to meet needs, not just saved for the future. The church developed a brochure that outlines their vision and the specifics of how they choose to handle money. It reads, "We strive to seek God, not money. We seek to surrender to God's will, listen to him and his direction, and then do what he says. Sometimes he tells us to do some pretty crazy things. And frankly, we don't always know from where the resources will come. And that leads us to another topic, called 'faith.' As we continue to understand God's views on money, we find we continue to learn more about obedience and faith. And the result continues to be celebration."

Clear statements like this guide church leaders in making decisions, but they also helpfully communicate the core values of the church. Until a thought, idea, or opinion is articulated, it's nothing more than a good idea. It can't be defended or changed. Churches must learn to communicate what they believe about money and generosity, explicitly letting others know that generosity is one of their core values. This also opens up opportunities for conversation and sets the expectations for new members who are just entering the community. It serves as an invitation to them, saying, "If you want to identify with us, then we invite you to share in this commitment with us."

Culture Weaves a Common Thread

While there will be times in the life of a church to focus on special giving opportunities for mission work, on-campus improvements, church planting, or multisite expansion, those aren't the only times to talk or think about generosity. The spirit and practice of generosity is always an outward sign of an inward commitment. It is the appropriate response of a person who has fully embraced the grace we have through our Lord Jesus Christ and his sacrifice for us on the cross. Just as we point to our personal checkbooks as evidence of what we value, the church must look at its own financial habits and determine whether it is holding itself accountable in the same way.

When Kent Sparks, pastor at the Argyle, Texas, campus of Cross Timbers Church, stood up before the congregation on a Sunday morning in October 2008, he didn't have to tell them that the economy was suffering. Many of the people in front of him had their own stories to tell or knew of friends and loved ones who were struggling to make ends meet. So Kent decided to take a bold step as he introduced the morning offering. "I just wonder if there is someone in this room who ought to receive, not give, today," Kent said. "Maybe someone here doesn't even have gas money to get home. If you're in that type of need, would you raise your hand?" A young, single mother in the congregation slowly raised her hand. When she did, Kent didn't just pray for her. He didn't suggest she apply for the church's benevolence fund. Instead he immediately walked down the aisle, took the twenty dollars he had in his wallet, and gave it to her. As soon as he did, others seated nearby opened their wallets and quickly, quietly, lovingly gave her even more money. In that simple act, a young family was blessed, and an entire congregation saw the power of bold, generous giving.

As with the good people at Cross Timbers, the evidence of a generous culture will often be visible in the weekend gatherings, but it should also be seen in the content of the church bulletin, in the language of giving on the church website, in the capacity of the church's people to meet the ministry demands of the community, and in the creative ways in which the church gives to others without an expectation of anything in return. It will also be evident in the personal habits and practices of the church leadership.

The clearest evidence of a generous church is a willingness to give that flows naturally from hearts touched by the grace of God. To an outsider, this type of generosity can seem reckless. It's similar to the generosity the Macedonian people practiced as described by Paul in 2 Corinthians 8:1–5: "Brothers and sisters, we want you to know about the grace that God has given the Macedonian churches. In the midst of a very severe trial, their overflowing joy and their extreme poverty welled up in rich generosity. For I testify that they gave as much as they were able, and even beyond their ability. Entirely on their own, they urgently pleaded with us for the privilege of sharing in this service to the Lord's people. And they exceeded our expectations: They gave themselves first of all to the Lord, and then by the will of God also to us."

The Macedonian church gave willingly and freely, pleading for the opportunity to share what they had with others. They saw giving as an opportunity and, despite their own poverty and need, gave joyfully. As Paul suggests, they were "rich" in generosity, exceeding expectations. As leaders of God's church, our greatest responsibility is to create an environment in which people can give like this. When people in our churches have an encounter with the living God and are touched by his grace, we find no greater evidence of God's power than the existence of a culture of reckless generosity. Generosity like this is exceptional, unexpected, and provides a clear witness to the transforming power of God.

Becoming a generous community, like the Macedonian church, doesn't happen overnight. It is necessary to cultivate the culture, communicate core values, challenge people with clear opportunities, and embed the vision for generosity in every area of life and ministry. The culture of your church is the foundation on which God will release his resources in his way to accomplish his plan.

In the end, the primary goal when creating a generous culture in your church is not financial gain or expansion of your budget. In fact, the real goal has very little to do with money. The real goal is spiritual formation. We believe that generous giving is one of the best external indicators for measuring transformation and spiritual growth. Paying attention to the giving habits of our faith communities gives us concrete feedback about the effectiveness of our discipleship strategies. That's why we want to emphasize that this is about raising up people, not simply raising money. You can raise money while raising up people, training and discipling them, but you can't raise up people by merely trying to raise money.

If all we had hoped to do was to help you raise more money, then we'd have written a different book. Instead we want to give you the means to help you normalize the conversation about faith and money. Additionally, we want to help you formulate a new way of thinking about money in church — not as a means by which we benefit ourselves and our churches but as the means by which we transform lives, and our communities, as the fruit of God's gracious love for us in Christ.

Key Ideas

- Culture represents a church's customs and attitudes. It answers the question, How do we do things around here?
- Culture is never neutral; it is either permitting or limiting.
- Culture is organic and develops even when the leader is not on the platform.
- Generosity is systemic. It should be a process that encompasses all aspects of church life, not a onetime effort.
- Well-executed tactics fail if there is no culture of generosity to support them.
- The culture of your church is as important as the vision for the church.
- There is no status quo; your church is either becoming more generous or less generous.

Discussion Questions

1. Through what lens is your church looking? What do outsiders see as important to your congregation?
2. Would you describe the culture of your church as generous?
3. Does culture trump vision in your church? If so, how? If not, why?
4. How has your church responded with unexpected generosity in the past?
5. How and when do you talk about generosity in your church?
6. In what ways are you providing the right conditions for your church to grow in its understanding and practice of generosity?

Chapter 2

GOOD STRATEGY IS BETTER THAN GOOD INTENTIONS

> The road to generosity is a journey that few Christians successfully complete. Some never get started on the journey.
> — *Walter B. Russell*

Church leaders who focus on generous giving find that once-a-year pledges or capital campaigns don't do enough to truly develop the lifestyle they want to see reproduced in their people. Leaders need practical, focused tools to teach the principles and practices of a generous life; without them, church members likely will remain unchanged in this matter of the heart.

"We have never shied away from talking about money," says Terry Busch, executive pastor of Centre Street Evangelical Missionary Church in Calgary. "However, I think we've frustrated people by talking about what they could do and should do, without giving them the tools they need to learn how to do those things."

For church leaders who echo Terry's sentiments, there is good news. The storehouse of tools to teach generous giving and biblical stewardship is rapidly expanding—with solid off-the-shelf resources that are being refined to meet the needs of modern-day churchgoers.

Churches that are ahead of the curve in developing the teaching component of a generous culture start their teaching at the top, with staff and leaders. And they address a full spectrum of needs—from people in financial crisis to the wealthiest individuals, and the 80 percent in between.

Strategy versus Intention

People often have good intentions. The church is full of good intentions. But in the midst of our coulds, shoulds, and oughts, we sometimes, for a variety of reasons, don't put our plans into action. We mean well. We want to take care of the poor, the hungry, and the widows, but sometimes life just gets in the way. We have small groups or Sunday school lessons to prepare, we have discipleship programs to plan, we have mission trips to coordinate, and we have outreach events and community events to promote.

And then a financial crisis comes, and our good intentions are put on hold again. Our moments of inspiration never become more than dreams discussed in passing. Somehow we just never seem to put those essential things—like generosity—into motion. Maybe our church does a good job of promoting missional activities, but without a generosity strategy, our ability to put our words into action and achieve measurable results will be hit or miss.

The key to a successful strategy is simple: establish a plan and then execute it. We tend to talk about our plan. We may pray about our plan, and that is essential. But at some point, we must establish specific, measurable steps, appoint the person who will lead the charge, and make it happen. Strategy leads to specific action steps that make a difference. Good intentions, on the other hand, lead to passivity. We satisfy our own need to feel good about ourselves, but good intentions lead to no quantifiable impact on the world.

Jesus is very clear that having a strategy that we follow through on is a vital part of true faith. He tells his disciples, "Suppose one of you wants to build a tower. Won't you first sit down and estimate the cost to see if you have enough money to complete it? For if you lay the foundation and are not able to finish it, everyone who sees it will ridicule you, saying, 'This person began to build and wasn't able to finish.' Or suppose a king is about to go to war against another king. Won't he first sit down and consider whether he is able with ten thousand men to oppose the one coming against him with twenty thousand?" (Luke 14:28–31).

Jesus understands that before trying to do something significant, we should first pause to consider the cost of achieving whatever goal we have in mind. In this passage, Jesus wants people to grasp what it really means to become his disciple and follow him, and be ready to do what it takes to make that happen. In a similar way, we must learn to craft a strategy for generosity and implement a plan to make it happen. If establishing a strategy and working out a plan is not part of our efforts and we find ourselves in that vague place of good intentions, just hoping something happens, then we are failing to follow Jesus' teachings. Our good intentions have led us to a place of disobedience and failure.

The main reason why some churches experience an abundance of resources is because they have a plan. They actively create a culture of generosity, and they execute their plan consistently. This doesn't mean that they always get it right or that everything they do stays the same forever. There are times of correcting the course along the way. But they have a bias toward action, and they do what they say they will do.

We can easily convince ourselves that our good intentions will become good strategy if we think and talk about them long enough. That's like thinking about exercise and expecting to produce the same benefit that exercising produces. Wouldn't that be nice! We all know that a tried-and-true plan of eating right and exercising, faithfully executed, is the best way to achieve good health. Likewise, no amount of hoping for generosity can produce measurable results within a community of believers. Even in cases in which a congregation is encouraged to be generous by a pressing need or an inspiring story, that generosity will wane without an intentional strategy to build and sustain a culture.

The leadership of Lincoln Berean Church in Lincoln, Nebraska, struggled through this very issue. "Guiding people to this principle of furthering God's agenda and not our own can be challenging; it's countercultural," says Brad Brestel, the church's stewardship pastor. "The image that lives with me, though, is that the rich young ruler walked away from Jesus sad. That isn't something I want for the people in my church."

Before Brad joined the staff at Lincoln, the church never talked about money. "It was a conscious choice that grew out of the televangelist scandals of the 1990s," he says. "Our elders wanted to set us apart from 'those guys.' In an attempt to avoid even an appearance of impropriety, they unintentionally created a vacuum, leaving our people with no biblical teaching on money." In 2003, the elders recognized the mistake they had made, and though they didn't want to pound people over the head about money, they wanted to correct course and return to a more biblical emphasis. Nearly overnight they rolled out a stewardship ministry. "They announced they had hired me as the stewardship pastor, and then they announced a capital campaign, almost in the same breath. God was ready, the people were ready, and the leaders had heard from God. Our giving had been tired, and just with these announcements, the giving went up 60 percent. We really taught lifestyle change rather than promoting a building campaign. Every month, giving went up, and we have been trying to keep up with God all the way."

How Far Does Generosity Reach?

Generosity touches every aspect of ministry in a church. It has a role to play in small groups, campus events, mission projects, our events and programming, and our celebration of changed lives. And when we talk about the comprehensive nature of generosity, we also mean that it must permeate every area of our leadership too. There is no part of how we do church—even our personal financial decisions as leaders—that shouldn't be impacted by a holistic understanding and discipline of generosity.

The first step for many churches is simply to define stewardship. "We had to decide, is stewardship about discipling and teaching, or is it about fundraising and development?" says Larry Powell, president of a private equity investment company in Atlanta and a lay leader at North Point Ministries. "We asked ourselves this question: If we are instructing our people about stewardship, and we see that their money is going elsewhere, not just to the church, is that okay? If the answer is yes, then we are approaching this as discipleship and teaching. If seeing the money go elsewhere isn't okay, then really all we are doing is fundraising. The conclusion we came to is that we want congregational giving to go up across the board—not just to the church but to other organizations as well. We want to see other totals go up. That's when we are doing our jobs as church leaders."

Sometimes we see churches with great intentions place the burden of stewardship and generosity on people tasked to oversee the finances of the church or organization. But doing this restricts the vision for generosity to the area of budgets and operational management, a limitation that makes it difficult for other leaders—the children's pastor, youth pastor, missions pastor, or spiritual formation pastor—to embrace generosity as a core value in their own ministries.

This deficiency becomes clear to us whenever we ask children's ministry leaders in various churches how they include generosity as part of their overall educational objectives. As children grow, most children's ministry leaders are careful to expose them to all the core doctrines of the faith. So when we ask these leaders to explain their teaching on prayer, Bible study, and worship, the answers they give are usually quite specific and well articulated. More often than not, however, when we ask leaders to share how they disciple children in the biblical teaching on generosity, you can almost hear a pin drop. Leaders aren't prepared to discuss this issue, let alone teach it to the children in their ministry.

Generosity is systemic. This means it's not a onetime effort or a passing event. It is a value that is taught and built right into the fabric of a church. It is a thread that runs through the entire organization and may at times become the focal point of the congregation, bringing unity and focus to every aspect of church life. For example, if we notice that we have a large number of people participating in new-member programs but a very small number of first-time givers, we may need to consider revisiting our new-member programming to ensure that we are communicating a churchwide commitment to generosity, one that clearly establishes it as an expectation for new members. Or if we notice that the number of our core givers peaks at age forty and begins to decline and flatline around age fifty-five, then we know that we are not capturing the hearts of couples with grown children.

Strategically Staffing for Generosity

One way in which some churches have strategically planned to encourage a culture of generosity is through intentional staffing decisions. Some churches have begun addressing this need by funding a staff position for a generosity or stewardship pastor. Even if the person filling this role isn't dedicated full-time to issues related to stewardship and generosity, he or she is often called on to champion the efforts of the church in this area. "Increasingly, innovative churches are hiring full-time staff members to execute the important role of developing ministries that lead people into the freedom of stewardship and joy of generosity," says Byron Van Kley, a former vice president of Generous Giving who helped to covene the first Generous Churches Leadership Community for Leadership Network. "The stewardship pastor position is gaining rapid adoption in larger churches. This staff position gives oversight to maturing the congregation spiritually with respect to financial stewardship." We believe that this surge in the number of stewardship pastors can be explained by the fact that effective churches are becoming more intentional about helping the congregation develop mature perspectives on money and giving. Many of those stewardship pastors are linking together through Christian Stewardship Network (CSN) for encouragement and sharing of ideas.

Those churches that have a dedicated stewardship staff member resoundingly affirm this position's role in advancing generosity in their congregations. While having this position doesn't excuse the lead pastor from teaching on generosity, it ensures that a constant strategy is being established, executed, and evaluated. Another approach that many churches have followed is to add these responsibilities to those of an existing staff member, such as the executive pastor, the business administrator, or the education pastor. Other churches appoint a committee or specific group of individuals to help lead this effort. Sometimes this committee or team is appointed by the larger body, and sometimes the members are handpicked by senior-level staff or the pastor himself. It is always desirable to have lay involvement, and such a team has functioned very effectively in many churches. Regardless of how an organization chooses to move forward, what matters is finding someone — an individual or a group in the church or ministry — who will own the responsibility and be the champion of seeing it through. Still, we must remember that just because a responsibility appears on a job description, that doesn't mean we're done and it's covered. Whoever is appointed to carry this responsibility must also be held accountable for results.

NorthRidge Church in Plymouth, Michigan, realized they would need a staff person to focus on generosity development. In 2005, Mike Miller, a volunteer leader in the church, began serving part-time on staff, with a focus on generosity and stewardship. Mike's job was moved to full-time in 2007. Shortly thereafter NorthRidge joined one of the Generous Church Leadership Communities facilitated by Leadership Network. The result was transformational for the church. They began to ask the question, "Who is NorthRidge Church in our community?" They realized that the best answer they could give was, "A big church." They also realized that they wanted to be known as a generous church, and they began the process of changing that impression.

In addition, NorthRidge Church realized that there was a missing piece: compassion. The first step they took to address this problem was to disciple their congregation. In other words, let's teach our people to match their walk and talk. The next step was to connect generosity to compassion. In other words, generosity funds compassion. As a result, in February 2011 the church took a special compassion offering and received more than $550,000. Shortly thereafter the church took another special offering and received $230,000 to team up with Feed My Starving Children in order to pack more than one million meals for kids in Haiti, Guatemala, and Somalia. The offering more than covered the million meals and exceeded the amount by so much that more than two hundred thousand extra meals were distributed among people in need in Mexico, through a partner church in Laredo, Texas. In the words of Mike Miller, "Bottom line, in the wake of the financial meltdown that hurt Michigan terribly, we invested more outside our walls than ever before, all while experiencing a small increase in our general fund. It seems God really smiled on our faithfulness."

Miller says the decision to participate in the Generous Church Leadership Community was the catalyst for defining the role of the generosity or stewardship pastor. It allowed their church to interface with other leaders and hear different ideas on developing generosity in the church. A key learning, according to Miller, was, "You can't develop culture from the generosity and stewardship office of the church. It has to be a thread that runs through all the other departments. You cannot do it in a silo. It has to be integrated into everything."

Aspects of Developing a Comprehensive Strategy

There are three aspects to developing a comprehensive strategy for promoting generosity and stewardship in a church: information, application, and transformation. Combined, these three have a cumulative effect that can lead to a huge impact on the church culture, but separated from one other, they will limit your effectiveness.

Information

The first aspect of strategy is information. Don't assume that your church members have a basic knowledge of generosity or stewardship. Leaders must take steps to ensure that everyone shares a fundamental level of information about and awareness of the subject. If you are leading a traditional church, *stewardship* may be a familiar word to some, but *generosity* may not. One of the first things you can do is to spend some time reviewing the numerous biblical passages that are relevant to these themes, developing a broader understanding of our calling to live generously rather than simply checking the box and paying our "fair share." Small group studies and personal testimonies are always very effective in communicating this type of information.

If you are leading a more contemporary or missional church, the word *generosity* may be familiar but may not be grounded in a biblical understanding of stewardship. And if your church has lots of new believers who don't come from church backgrounds, the words *stewardship* and *generosity* may mean nothing to them. If this is the case, the best way to start is to introduce the subject. This can be done from the platform, through an annual giving emphasis or a preaching series, or it can be done in another way, perhaps through a small group study. Don't forget to repeatedly communicate to your church members the process behind assembling budgets and organizational goals, and highlight any measurable life change you've witnessed as a result of the church's generosity. Draw attention to the ministries that you, as a church, are investing in for the future. Communication like this helps build trust and confidence in the leadership's ability to manage and multiply the gifts given to expand the kingdom through the ministry of your church.

Application

Information alone doesn't lead to transformation. You also need application. Application requires a call to action. You can begin by setting up expectations — perhaps a certain percentage of giving — for your new and existing members. The key is not so much where you start; it's remembering to constantly challenge people to take the next step, no matter where they are on their journey. If a person is giving nothing right now, you can urge them to give 1 percent. If they are currently giving a tithe, or 10 percent, you can encourage them to begin giving 11 percent. Small, manageable steps provide immediate ways of applying the information you are communicating.

Generous churches also place a premium on creative strategies, tools, and resources to spread the message of giving. And they make certain their generosity goals are filtering through to the congregation. For example, Asbury United Methodist Church has built its ministry around eight core objectives.

1. Every member confessing Jesus Christ as Lord.
2. Every member living to love, seek, and save the lost through Christ.

3. Every member worshiping God, corporately and privately.
4. Every member participating in a small group Christian community.
5. Every member developing a biblical worldview by learning and applying God's Word.
6. Every member bringing the tithe (one-tenth) in loving obedience to God's gracious provision.
7. Every member devoted to prayer.
8. Every member discovering and using spiritual gifts for ministry and mission.

While your church may have articulated your list of objectives differently, you can see how language like this, put into action, can shape the life of a believer and a church. Over the years, Asbury had developed significant action plans for seven of the eight objectives. Interestingly enough, only number 6—the giving objective—lacked a clear, specific plan for action. When the leaders realized this, they got busy creating one. They decided to give greater emphasis to *Financial Peace University*, an educational and discipleship curriculum they had been running for several years. The church also made a decision to hire a stewardship pastor, Jim Lenderman, and gave him the charge to develop new ways of incorporating stewardship into Asbury's educational programs. Jim began investigating the idea of something called a "discovery ministry," in which people could explore local opportunities to get their hands dirty and learn how their time, their talents, and their treasure could best be put to use.

WoodsEdge Community Church in Spring, Texas, faced a slightly different problem than did the folks at Asbury. WoodsEdge had long had a host of tools and resources to encourage generous living, but executive pastor Ken Williams realized that, unfortunately, the congregation was largely unaware of these resources. "Unless someone had needed and sought out a certain kind of support in the past," Ken says, "it became pretty obvious that they had no idea of what our church offered. With the economic downturn deepening, I knew we needed to be more proactive in getting the word out." The church started informing people about certain resources before they were requested, promoting them as great tools for discipleship and spiritual growth.

However you choose to apply what you teach, our point is simple: intentions don't become reality without a call to some type of action. While secular nonprofit organizations and parachurch ministries have become adept at presenting compelling calls to action, churches often neglect such practices because they feel it is wrong or improper to put too much emphasis on asking for money. We would suggest that churches need to take a cue from these organizations and begin calling their members to action. Calling people to action, when it is based on biblical truth, is a necessary aspect of discipleship. We truly learn what we know when we apply what we know. Our churches are filled with people who think they know what it means to be generous, but until they are challenged to put their thinking into action, those thoughts are just ideas and good intentions. So how is your church calling others to practice contagious, reckless generosity? Application is often the missing link—a step that is easily overlooked—in the process of learning what it means to be generous.

Application also separates the people who talk from the people who act, an important distinction when you fill leadership roles and identify pillars of influence in your church. When we are given the opportunity to analyze the giving habits of a church's members, we often take a close look at people in the top positions of leadership. Many pastors are surprised to learn who are the top givers and who aren't. Often, a pastor will think that he has been listening to the voice of a faithful giver, only to learn that he has not. Of course, a pastor should not show favoritism, but having some information about giving habits can reveal which church leaders are stepping out in faith to help accomplish the mission and which are not.

Transformation

Only after we've established a common level of knowledge and given a consistent call to action so that this knowledge is applied can we begin to expect transformation to occur. However, we must be aware that we cannot control the process of transformation. It's impossible to predict what transformation will look like, and we can't always be sure of the outcome. Still, while we can't control it, anticipate it, or completely measure its impact, leaders usually can recognize life change when it happens. We must not forget that transformation begins in the heart. We first recognize it in subtle ways: the prompting of the Holy Spirit that leads to a spontaneous act, stretching a person to sacrifice beyond expectation. It may be seen in a community of believers who work together, putting aside their own self-interest to achieve more collectively than they could individually. We may recognize it when people start making significant modifications to their lifestyle, outlook, and goals. Knowledge of the Scriptures fused with regular challenges to apply what we value and believe can spark a blaze of generosity. And when the fires are burning throughout our church, we know that genuine transformation has occurred.

The fruit of transformation looks different in every church. Some churches begin hosting reverse offerings, allowing people in need to take from the offering plate. Others choose to distribute funds to their members and encourage them to find someone in need to give the money to. Some churches choose simply to give all of their money away, even when that puts them in a vulnerable place financially.

Authentic transformation will never be safe. It will always cost us something, but because we know that God is good and is in control, we know that it will make an eternal difference. When God shows up in someone's life and changes his or her money habits, the impossible somehow becomes possible. Our love for comfort and security based on what we buy and own is replaced with a newfound freedom to generously share what has been given to us. It doesn't matter if the person being transformed is a single mom with little children or a bachelor millionaire—transformation leads to freedom and is a clear sign that God is at work.

It Doesn't Matter Where You Begin

No matter where you are today in your personal or corporate journey toward living generously, you can start right where you are. Some new churches include generosity as a core value from the moment they launch, while other, more established churches adopt the value of generosity later, integrating it into every aspect of their life as a community. Wherever you are in this journey, and wherever your church is now, the key is to begin where you are. This starts with assessing your current situation.

Get to know your people. Spend time asking questions and understanding your church's culture. Learn how your volunteer leadership talks about and thinks about their personal finances, how they handle money. Review the giving habits of your staff. Listen to people in your new-member classes and, if possible, follow up with them a few months later to see if being involved in the church has had an impact on their behavior. You may even consider asking someone outside your church to offer a more objective, thorough analysis of your church and your current culture of generosity. The quality of your assessment will go a long way toward determining the effectiveness of your plan.

You Don't Have to Do Everything; Just Do *Something*

When we craft a strategy for creating a culture of generosity, we often build it on the assumption of economic growth and prosperity. But what happens when that isn't the case?

Northland, A Church Distributed, in Longwood, Florida, has a long history of collaborating and generously sharing with the church of Christ that is distributed throughout the world. Hence their unique name. But even though this passion to share has long been a part of the church's story, the leaders recognized that they did not have a plan to see that passion for generosity filter down to the congregation and become a part of the culture. That need was vividly revealed during the recent economic meltdown. Under the leadership of executive director of operations Marc McMurrin, and with the enthusiastic support of senior pastor Joel Hunter and the elders and staff, Northland put together a comprehensive generosity plan that included budget counseling, estate planning and will seminars, sermon series, and the launching of five hundred new *Financial Peace University* groups to teach congregants the much-needed basics of financial stewardship. The results were stunning. Giving increased from 92 percent of the budget in 2010 to 99 percent of the budget in 2011, even in the midst of a down economy.

We can learn from churches that have adopted a clear strategy to develop generosity, instead of relying on good intentions and favorable financial circumstances. These were churches that talked about their goals. They combined knowledge with application and are now showing signs of transformation. The leaders of these churches practiced generosity and set the expectation for all staff members. They made commitments and reworked financial obligations to ensure that the generosity of their congregations would benefit hurting people in their community and around the world.

They knew what to do. They were prepared. And God blessed their efforts. We realize that you, as a leader, have more to focus on in your ministry than creating a culture of generosity in your church. Through the years, we've interacted with numerous leaders who have been overwhelmed by all they have to do. Growing discouraged, they eventually abandon the goal of cultivating generosity. The good news is that if you're feeling at all like that right now, you're not alone! The other good news we have for you is that we're just getting started. As you work through the remaining chapters, we hope you'll pick up ideas that will be easy to implement. We want to encourage you to write those down somewhere and begin putting them into action — right away. You don't have to have everything together before you start. What matters, however, is that you get started. Remember that even the greatest champions of generosity didn't start where they are today. They had to learn too. And if they had to learn, that means it's also possible for you and your church to become a community of contagious generosity.

Key Ideas

- Hope is not a good strategy. Neither is "want to" or "plan to." Busyness isn't good strategy either.
- Staff appropriately for generosity leadership. Someone needs to own it.
- Strategy is both informational and transformational. There are some things that you need to know, but information alone doesn't lead to transformation. Information plus application equals transformation.
- It matters more that you start than where you begin.
- You don't have to do everything, but you do have to do something.
- Generosity strategy is less like fundraising and more like spiritual formation.
- What areas need to be included? Small groups, coaching, leadership development, planned giving, preaching—*everything*!
- Churches must have a plan for all seasons, good and bad.

Discussion Questions

1. What is your strategy for developing a culture of generosity in your church?
2. Can you describe your church's comprehensive spiritual formation plan? Is generosity part of that plan? If not, how will you include it?
3. Have you limited conversations about money in church to times of need or crisis?
4. Reflect on your church's generosity habits over the past two years. What can you learn? How will (or should) that shape your strategy moving forward?
5. How are you relying on information to inspire generosity, and are you providing opportunities for people to practice generosity?

6. How are you moving people along the generosity journey in a way that puts spiritual formation at the forefront of the process?

7. How has your strategy changed through different stages in the life of your church? What has worked at one time that didn't work again (or vice versa)?

Chapter 3

GENEROSITY IS CONTAGIOUS

True giving is not an economic exchange; it is a generative act. It does not subtract from what we have; it multiples the effect we can have in the world. —*Kent Nerburn*

If there is one behavior that constantly surprises people, it is the act of generosity. We both travel a lot. We tip hotel staff and even help out people we meet along the way. Sometimes we choose to do this well beyond expectations. We don't do this because we have been blessed with an abundance of financial resources. Nor do we do it just because we want to feel better about ourselves. We love to give, because giving is an opportunity to pass along the joy of our faith in Christ. We share with others in a way that has been modeled for us by other believers and by the God who gave himself for us.

The greatest way to change the world, Gandhi once said, is to *be* the change we wish to see in the world. We believe that this wisdom gets at one of the key reasons why generosity is contagious. When we are generous, it creates an experience that leaves both the giver and the recipient different than they were. We can stand by and watch other people giving generously and be inspired by their actions. But when we ourselves choose to give freely, not only is monetary currency exchanged, but also an intangible currency is passed from recipient to giver, a currency so powerful that it inspires both people to form the habit of giving.

When a church operates out of the belief that there are limited resources for the work of ministry, it operates at less than full capacity. It places limits on the dreams that are pursued. It restricts the ability of its people to think beyond what is currently believed to be possible. It minimizes ministry potential to the limits of available resources. This creates a "scarcity" mindset, rooted in a fear that one day we will run out of resources. Worse, when church leaders operate with this sense of scarcity, their behavior trickles down to the person in the pew. During recent times of recession, we heard many leaders talk about holding on to what they had. Sadly, we saw some congregations embrace their financial fears and stifle their faith. Instead of asking what God might do in the midst of challenging economic circumstances and dreaming up new opportunities to proclaim Christ, they limited their dreams by cutting budgets and scaling back ministry — and limited their potential for spiritual growth and community impact.

Churches that practice a contagious level of generosity don't see or acknowledge limits. They begin with a foundational belief that we serve an all-powerful, all-knowing, and always-present God who creates resources when they don't exist. Contagious giving is rooted in faith, and it remains open to the impossible. The paramount question is not, What do we need to cut to survive? It is, What is God calling us to do next? If the God we serve is not bound by our human limitations, then he certainly isn't limited by our cash flow — or lack of it! We must remember that when God calls us to do something, he has already equipped us with the resources we need to do what he asks of us — even if that means depending on him and growing in our faith.

The Cure for Scarcity

The most practical way to cure the cancer of the scarcity mindset is to simply let go. Open up the checkbook. Begin to release the funds that your church has been saving for a rainy day. To be clear, we are not suggesting that you throw common sense to the wind and act foolishly in financial matters. We are advocating that you take some healthy steps of faith, taking risks to create opportunities for God to respond to your need. Contagious generosity always carries with it a certain sense of recklessness that trusts God, saying, "There's more where that came from." And this radical generosity is the path to truly curing the scarcity mindset.

Consider how God tested Abraham's faith in the book of Genesis. God had miraculously given Abraham a son, named Isaac, in his old age. This was the fulfillment of God's promise. To test Abraham's faith, God asked him to sacrifice Isaac. This was a significant moment for three reasons. First of all, Isaac was Abraham's son, whom he loved. Second, the sacrifice of another person was a highly unusual request from God. Third, Isaac was the only proof Abraham had that God would honor his promise to make Abraham the father of many nations. Abraham was faced with a test of obedience: would he eliminate the only connection he had to the divine commitment? Of course, Abraham didn't end up having to sacrifice his son. God provided a ram instead. But Abraham's obedience—his willingness to step out and trust God to provide for him—was honored by God and proved Abraham's worthiness to be the father of many nations. Abraham would not be the model of faith for us today if he had not chosen to be obedient to God.

The same is true for us as leaders in the church. We may feel at times that heeding the call to be a generous church is unwise. It defies common sense. It will be too much for our church to endure. After all, there is barely enough to go around now! When we feel this way, we need to recognize that God is inviting us to answer his call, to take steps of obedience and give generously. Just as God provided a ram to Abraham, so God will provide for our needs when we follow his commands and step out in faith and in obedience to his call.

When we acknowledge that God is the owner of all things—even the resources we have been given as stewards—then we have no choice but to willingly share what we have with others. To live as imitators of Christ, as Paul admonishes us to do (1 Thess. 1:6; 2:14), we must be willing to give up the feeling of security that comes from thinking we have control over our future. Faith in God's future for us empowers us with hope and life that we can then share with others.

Not Giving to Receive

At this point, however, we want to clarify one thing: when we talk about stepping out in faith and giving generously, we are not talking about a health-and-wealth theology. There is no give-to-get strategy here. The health-and-wealth mentality—giving in order to receive—simply does not match what the Bible teaches us about God's economy. Our giving is to be motivated by the gospel of God's grace, not by an expectation of getting something in return. The grace of God provided for us in Jesus Christ is sufficient to meet all of our needs. We give not because we hope to gain additional resources but because God has given freely to us.

That said, it is also true that when we give freely in this way, we have access to a deep well of life that offers us many things in return. Sometimes our act of giving offers freedom from our deepest fears. Sometimes it brings us great joy. And sometimes God does provide additional financial resources. But those blessings are never the goal of our giving. They do not motivate our hearts to give that we might receive a blessing in return. Whenever we make what we receive the goal of our giving, we reveal the power of consumerism over our hearts and minds. Giving in this way is simply a repackaging of our selfish desires so they have the appearance of generosity; it's not a true reflection of God's gracious love for us.

In the same way that God freely gave of himself, with no expectation of anything in return, churches should also be willing and eager to freely give to people in need. Time after time, we have seen the grace of God lived out in this way. We've seen pastors request cuts in their own salaries to avoid frontline ministry staff layoffs. We've seen churches spend their reserve funds to help people in need in their communities. And we've seen churches choose to operate on a lean budget in order to create additional margin so they can give away money to mission work.

None of these steps were taken because they were easy or comfortable or because there was a hidden motive to receive more money in return. There was no selfish intent in these sacrificial acts of generosity. But in each of these churches, as they responded in step with the gracious and generous nature of God, we saw evidence of God's blessings. We saw churches that had plateaued in their spiritual fervor blaze brightly once again. We saw staff on the verge of burnout reignited with a passion for ministry. And we saw churches scared of losing everything they owned receive increased contributions and special gifts — and a newfound confidence in God's love for them. Though none of these blessings were guaranteed or sought, they confirm that God provides for his people when they trust him with their needs.

Making It Obvious

In early 2009, Cross Timbers Community Church was suffering from the effects of the economic meltdown. Offerings were low and the board was wrestling with how to bridge the gap between current offerings and the ministry budget. The obvious solution was to make cuts in ministry expenses. Donations at the church had slumped because of the economy, and Pastor Toby Slough knew that the people of Cross Timbers had to be hurting too. So Toby met with the board, sharing with them his belief that God wanted them to give away the money they had to hurting people in their community. He wasn't suggesting that they make an appeal for funds; in fact, he was suggesting that they give away much of the money they had in their reserve fund.

That following week, the church passed around the collection plate and told the congregation that if anyone had a need, they were to feel free to take money from the plate instead of giving to it. Amazingly, the offering that week was significantly higher than the previous weeks' had been. And in the two-month period following that Sunday, this nine-year-old church gave over a half million dollars to members and nonmembers who were struggling financially.

The decision to give rather than receive was met with an unexpected response: the offerings each week increased well above projections, surpassing the previous records for giving in the church. This was an aha moment for Pastor Slough. He and the other leaders of the church realized that if they gave away money to people who needed it, church members would help fill those needs. In other words, if they acted in a way consistent with their mission, trusting God to do the work, the congregation would respond. "Sometimes we can be so into the church 'business' that we forget what our real business is, and that is to help hurting people," Slough says.

The church began to look for creative ways to give money away during this season of generosity. "We took in two hundred thousand dollars and spread it out to organizations—four local, two missions that are feeding and clothing people in these tough times," Slough says. "We've paid utility bills for members of our church who are unemployed or underemployed." One week, the church gave back the entire offering to the members after the service in increments of fifty dollars, stipulating that they give it to someone in need. Members were also asked to post the stories of their giving on a website for the whole church to share. It was a powerful experience for everyone in the church. This is contagious generosity in action!

Churches that avoid talking about money from the pulpit or speak about it only once or twice a year still send a clear message about money to their people. Avoiding the issue sends the message that you think your people don't want you to talk about it. While that may seem like a solution, it makes the problem much worse, in that the church is validating wrong beliefs about faith and money. This is where we have to move strategically to normalize the conversation. In other words, make the conversation about faith and money so natural that people don't get uptight when it comes up. North Point Community Church in Alpharetta, Georgia, has done well in this area. When they have financial needs, they address the situation openly in church under the leadership of their pastor, Andy Stanley. Andy has said to his people many times, "Generosity is something we want *for* you, not *from* you." As a result, people don't get uptight and anxious, and the very bold ministry needs of this influential, growing church are met.

Churches also make a statement about money in the way they budget and spend. What does your giving, as a church body, say about your priorities and values as a congregation? How we use our money is more telling than nearly anything else we do. How we spend it says something about us. How we save it reveals our priorities. But we make the clearest statement of all when we give our money away. Churches must learn to recognize that if they're not being generous with the money God has entrusted to them, it's obvious to everyone. We can pretend to be many things, we can preach and teach on this subject of generosity, but it's nearly impossible to fool people into thinking you're a generous person. The only way to get people to think that of you is to act in ways that are visibly generous. The good news is that when we do live generously, it compels people outside the church to take a second look and reevaluate their orientation toward God, faith, and the church. Generous people share themselves and their resources with others in such a way that it invites others to live generously too.

Inspiring generosity in the lives of other people starts with you, as a leader. Generosity comes from within, out of the overflow of your heart. It is more than just another task on your agenda. Generosity is, at heart, a response to the gift of God's grace through Jesus Christ. As you spend time reflecting on the gospel, on what Christ has done for you, it awakens your heart to a new desire — to freely give what you have received in order to help others in need.

A pastor who practices generosity like this will have a contagious energy. Leaders, for better or for worse, tend to create within the congregation a reflection of their own personal habits. When church leaders embrace a commitment to practice corporate generosity and good stewardship, it encourages the members and challenges them to do the same. Creating a culture of generosity begins with the pastor and the core leadership and spreads from their example to the rest of the church. More about that in the next chapter.

The Details of Your Budget

It's easy to get distracted by doing church and forget what we are to focus on in the first place. Sometimes our efforts to follow good financial disciplines inhibit our ability to function as God intended. If a culture of generosity has one characteristic that fuels its contagious nature, it is this: generous churches believe that meeting needs is more important than balancing the budget.

Don't get us wrong; churches must diligently manage their resources in order to meet these needs on even greater levels. However, financial management should lead not to greater savings for ourselves tomorrow but rather to an increased ability to give away more today. Financial administrators should learn to see themselves as gateways — not gatekeepers — to the world of generosity. Again, this highlights a key idea we have been emphasizing in this chapter: if leaders embrace generosity, then the congregation will too.

A few days after celebrating the fulfillment of his church's funding goals, the executive pastor of one church we frequently work with walked into his office with a deep desire to help people in his community. By the end of the day, the staff had prayerfully decided to deplete the church's emergency fund. They realized that emergency funds were made for emergencies and that if there was ever a time of emergency, it was now. When the staff and the pastor communicated this decision to the congregation the next Sunday, it ignited a spirit of contagious generosity in the hearts of the people. They saw that their leaders weren't holding on to the emergency fund in a protective way. The decision to give made a statement about what the church truly valued, what it affirmed as the object of its ministry: the people of the community. That decision communicated a message as powerful as any sermon preached that day.

The decisions that a church makes at a corporate level will have a direct impact on the spiritual formation of its members. The church's spending habits are what build the trust needed to inspire generous living. People today demand more information from the organizations they support and from the leaders they follow, and the members of your church will want access to reliable data to ensure that the mission your church verbalizes matches how the church spends its money. Take some time to evaluate your church budget. Is there anything in your budget that, if revealed to your church body or to the larger community, would diminish your church's credibility?

Consider your payroll. What percentage of your budget goes toward payroll and administrative costs? What percentage toward programming and travel? Take an honest look at every category in your budget. If you find items in your budget that cannot be adequately explained, it may lead to questions that can erode trust in the leadership rather than build it.

We should also pay attention to people on the fringe in our churches, those who have not yet become members but are curious about the church, as well as those who aren't fully committed yet. Though we typically overlook these groups when considering financial decisions and budget planning, these are the people most likely to walk away from the church if they do not sense a commitment to generosity and kingdom priorities. Typically, these people are looking for the church to make an impact on the community and people. They aren't interested in well-funded traditions, burdensome administrative costs, retaining beloved staff members, or financing ineffective programming. They want to know that the money they give is being used to make a real-world difference. They want to know that what we do with our money matches what we say, that our actions support our stated values.

A good rule of thumb in this area is that everything in your budget is always on the table. If something worked in the past, that doesn't mean you should do it again. And if it didn't work in the past, that doesn't mean you should abandon it altogether. What matters most is that you are able to clearly explain your church's expenditures and show how the decisions you make align with your mission and lead to a measurable impact on the world. This takes work! When was the last time you considered the details of the budget, paying attention to where every dollar is spent? Sometimes the person in the congregation can uncover details that we aren't even aware of. As leaders, we need to be prepared to respond to questions and willing and ready to defend our budgeting choices. Because many people are cynical about the church today and don't always trust leaders in the way they allocate funds and spend money, we must avoid dismissing or ignoring questions that people raise. Instead we must work to cultivate an atmosphere of trust by being transparent and knowledgeable.

It can be a challenge to maintain objectivity in your decision making, and because of this, many churches seek outside help when analyzing their budgets. As a leader, are you willing to take an honest look at your church by inviting an outside voice to identify areas of discrepancy in your budget? Are you willing to listen and learn? Looking within is difficult. It's hard to admit where we may have made mistakes, and it takes work to make the necessary changes. The reality is that most organizations are in a state of flux, especially a growing and dynamic community, so we need to regularly evaluate our churches' habits to make sure they are in alignment with our values.

Accountability Encourages Generosity

When your church demonstrates good stewardship and financial accountability, members are more likely to trust you and follow that lead. At Cross Timbers Community Church, demonstrating financial accountability takes many forms.

- *Tracking.* Giving-per-attender statistics are monitored for each campus to uncover any changes, up or down.
- *Reserve fund.* Cross Timbers maintains reasonable liquidity, for both current and unexpected expenses. At any given time, the church may have upward of three to five months' worth of operating expenses in the bank.
- *Contingency plans.* When the economy showed early signs of trouble — even before the church's giving dipped — Cross Timbers prepared emergency plans that would be ready if needed.
- *"Family" meetings.* In congregational meetings, the staff reassures people that the church is keeping a close eye on its finances and will make whatever changes prove to be necessary.

- *Web-based information.* The church's website invites visitors to request a copy of the church's audit or call for more information at any time.

Asbury United Methodist Church has also found that financial transparency and accountability build trust. In Asbury's case, this started with strong financial leaders who offered the church some of the same financial controls with which they managed successful for-profit enterprises. Asbury's last two controllers have been CPAs. And the church's finance committee isn't composed merely of willing volunteers; rather it's composed of skilled business professionals who have experience building and managing complex financial systems. Executive director Dwight Yoder reports that all the church's finances are fully audited each year—a twenty-thousand-dollar annual investment but one that Dwight says is more than worth it.

And what happens when people see that you are being wise with the money they have given? Great things can happen. Dwight recalls receiving a call some time ago from one member. He had been blessed financially and was interested in giving more. He wanted to set up a meeting with Dwight to ask a simple question: "If I gave X amount to this church, where would it go? What would you do with it?" Dwight outlined the purposes toward which the money might be put and the financial controls that would ensure that the man's money would be well spent. This individual was so impressed—and so excited about the way his gift would be used—that he ended up giving twice the amount he originally had in mind!

Dwight believes in being transparent about Asbury's finances for one simple reason: "The money, after all, belongs to God, not the staff." Charles Stinson, a lay leader at Asbury, adds, "That type of transparency builds trust, and trust encourages personal generosity. Actually, these difficult times bring a huge opportunity for many members in our church. Because we are reasonably stable in what has become an unstable economy, we're thinking more and more about how to live and give."

Generosity beyond the Church

Although generosity may be cultivated primarily through the ministry of the church, we must never limit it to the budgetary decisions and programs of the church. Sometimes, being a generous community means relinquishing control of the dollar and sending it around the world, partnering with other like-minded ministries. God doesn't look at the church as a collection of 501(c)(3)s; he sees his children working together to mobilize for greater mission capacity and higher levels of ministry impact.

North Coast Church, a multisite church in California, has an intentional strategy for cultivating giving that does not rely on the church budget. The church tries to expose its congregation to different overseas missionaries and then invites the congregation to support these missionaries directly. In other words, the church tries to avoid being a middleman, preferring to cultivate a giving relationship directly between the people of the church and the missionary. Senior teaching pastor Larry Osborne and his team aren't worried about money leaving the church. In fact, they are thrilled to be used by God in this way, to connect missionaries with their supporters. "The only problem with this arrangement," Larry discloses, "is that it's impossible to do a good job of tracking the amount our people give to missions — in fact, we don't even try to track it. That's a small loss, though, in light of the benefits of allowing our missionaries to have a direct contact with those who are supporting them. It's helped our people have a broader mentality about the kingdom of God. It's organic, not bureaucratic."

North Coast teaching pastor Chris Brown believes that the more traditional "storehouse" perspective, in which the church collects the money and allocates it to different ministries and missionaries, once made sense but not any longer: "Before the internet and electronic communication, individuals didn't have many opportunities to relate to missionaries, so the storehouse function made sense. Today, though, virtually every person can communicate effectively, often, and instantly with those in ministry on the other side of the world. This way, missionaries can contact one hundred or two hundred people immediately to ask for prayer, instead of going through the church. That kind of personal relationship wasn't possible only a few years ago."

North Coast's ministry encourages every person in the church to let the Spirit guide them in making decisions about investing their time, energy, and funds. Chris explains, "From the beginning, Larry has wanted people to fall in love with Christ, trusting that the Spirit will change them from the inside out." The church's role is to encourage and challenge people to become followers of Christ, and expose them to real needs. It's up to the Spirit to motivate and lead people to get involved and give of their resources to meet those needs.

Some churches may see North Coast's lack of top-down control as a problem, but Larry, Chris, and the rest of the leaders continue to see people responding to the needs presented to them by giving generously and gladly. Citing a recent example, Chris says he was talking with a high-capacity donor, and the man told him about his son's involvement with an orphanage overseas. The man had donated money to help build a large chicken farm for the orphanage. The church would never have known about this man's gift if it hadn't been for this serendipitous conversation, but as Chris points out, "This act of generosity is just a part of what God is doing in and through people at North Coast."

Extending generosity beyond the church budget provides some balance to the tendency many leaders have to overemphasize the internal ministries of the church. It's tempting and easy for us to prioritize the ministries that we control and that directly affect us, becoming so focused on ourselves that we forget about other ministries and missionaries committed to spreading the gospel around the world.

Generosity Is Exciting!

Being generous should become part of our natural response to the grace of God. People who live generously treat their giving as they would any other aspect of life that they value—with intentionality. They willingly adjust their lifestyles because they are consumed with a heartfelt desire to share what they have with those in need. This motivates them to want to do more, to give more freely and generously to others.

Generosity is not an obligation; it's an opportunity for believers to be shaped into the image of Christ that people around them so desperately need. Generosity also reminds us that there is hope, even when our circumstances appear dark and grim. It draws us to look to God, and we are reminded that because we serve a God who creates out of nothing, the realm of possibility for our future is greater than we can ever imagine. Generous churches generate a positive energy that asks what God is calling us to do next, not what we can accomplish in our own strength and wisdom. Generous churches live with hands wide open, knowing that God is the source of all we have, are, and ever will become. The act of giving creates a contagious energy that draws people—even those with little or no faith—because it's authentic and unexpected. It's compelling evidence that God is at work.

Key Ideas

- People who practice what they believe exude a contagious energy.
- Your church's budget defines what's most important to your church, just as a checkbook reveals what is most important to a giver.
- Scarcity is a cancer. Generosity is the cure.
- If leaders embrace generosity, then the congregation will too.
- We do not give expecting to receive; we give because it is what God expects of us.
- Meeting the needs of the people in your church and community is more important than balancing your budget.
- Deciding how to use our resources isn't about what we are capable of accomplishing; it's about what God is calling us to do next.

Discussion Questions

1. When have you witnessed the giving story of one person inspiring generosity in another?
2. If the details of your church's budget were leaked, would it inspire people to give? Or would it raise a lot of questions?
3. Are there things in your church that model poor stewardship, such as an unproductive staff member?
4. What tough decisions are you postponing that—if executed—would allow you to increase your ministry capacity?
5. Are you leading your church with a belief in the abundance of resources, or are you leading it with a belief in their scarcity?
6. In what ways have you been contagious in leveraging your financial resources for ministry impact?

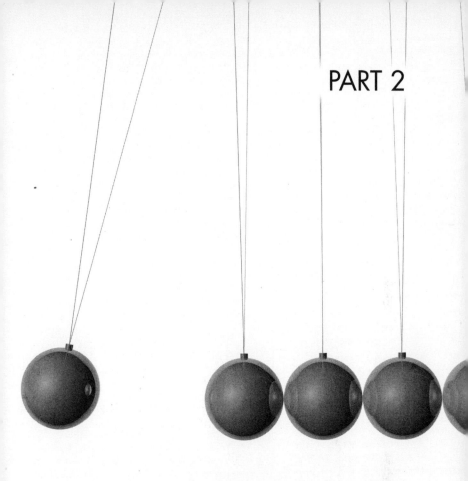

LEADERSHIP
DEVELOPMENT

Chapter 4

FOLLOW ME

To learn to be content, you must recognize God as the owner of all your possessions. If you believe you own even a single possession, then the circumstances affecting that possession will be reflected in your attitude.

—*Howard Dayton*

Generous churches are led by generous pastors. Period. It's possible to be a generous pastor of an ungenerous church. But we have never seen a generous church that is not led by a generous pastor. This speaks to the level of influence leaders have on their communities. In many cases we encounter, there is a direct relationship between a church that is struggling to stay alive financially and that church's pastor who is struggling with money issues.

We understand that as a pastor, you didn't commit your life to professional ministry because you wanted to talk about money. You may even have been trained to believe that talking about subjects such as money, sex, and politics were off-limits and potentially offensive. So we understand if you are reluctant to teach or preach on this subject. In fact, we want to start out by letting you know two things: (1) it's okay to be uncomfortable talking about money, and (2) it's not okay to let that discomfort become an excuse for failing to disciple your people in this area.

The truth is that leaders who lead generous churches don't just talk a good game. They have trained themselves in the principles of generosity, and they openly model a generous life. "Generosity is a value that is modeled at the top level," says one of Gateway Church's pastors, David Smith. "It's not just something we talk about; it is modeled on all levels—individuals, leaders, and as a church."

At Gateway Church in Southlake, Texas, another church that we have been privileged to work with over the years, this all starts with the senior pastor, Robert Morris. In his book *The Blessed Life: The Simple Secret of Achieving Guaranteed Financial Results* (Regal, 2004), Robert tells how his decision to model giving for his church began. As a young evangelist depending on freewill offerings to survive, Robert made a decision to give away his only offering check for the month. That same night, he was blessed to see God return it back to him tenfold! Robert goes on to share how during one eighteen-month period, he and his wife gave away nine vehicles they had received, only to have each one replaced by God. Robert also recounts how, on yet another occasion, he felt God telling him to give away both of his cars, his house, and all the money in his bank account. He writes, "I remember thinking to myself, 'Aha! I've got Him. This time I've outgiven the Lord!'" Then came God's response: a man called to tell Robert that he had purchased him an airplane and was going to pay for the hangar, fuel, insurance, maintenance, pilot, and any other traveling expenses. "As I stood there stammering and stunned, I heard the still, small voice of the Lord whisper in my spirit, 'Gotcha.'"

Not every pastor will be called by God to do what Robert did. And every pastor may not see the same types of blessings that Robert received, but we believe that a pastor's attitude about his own finances will have a direct effect on the community he serves. Frequently, churches we've worked with have experienced exceptional growth in giving when the pastor has spoken freely about his attitudes toward money. In other words, the posture you take in this matter will set the expectation and the tone for others. Your orientation toward generosity will inspire others to follow suit, or it will distract them from using what they have for the advancement of the kingdom.

Pastors and Money

Sam Crabtree is the executive pastor of Bethlehem Baptist Church in Minneapolis, Minnesota. Sam shared with us that senior pastor John Piper has consistently been the example and the inspiration for generosity at their church: "For his twenty-seven years at our church, John has been robustly God-focused and nonmaterialistic. When he has to replace his car, he only buys a used one. His books have sold in the millions, but he gives all the royalties away. In fact, his contract with publishers directs the money to go straight to a foundation that distributes the money. He never sees the checks. John says that he is frankly afraid of money's power of seduction."

Not surprisingly, Bethlehem's view of generosity is deeply rooted in the Scriptures. John teaches the supremacy of God in all things, including our finances. God created all things, and he reigns over all things. Sam often quotes Paul's summary statement about God's sovereignty at the end of Romans 11: "From him and through him and for him are all things. To him be the glory forever!"

In line with the vision taught and preached by their senior pastor, the ministries of Bethlehem recognize the devastating impact of consumerism on spiritual vitality, and they teach a deep and balanced approach that emphasizes wise stewardship of God's gifts. God, they explain, is incredibly generous to us in every way, and we are to "imitate him as beloved children" in our generosity. We have been given every spiritual blessing in Christ, but at the same time, financial prosperity isn't promised to us. It isn't a right that we are guaranteed in this life, nor is it something we can claim from God. On this side of heaven, we must learn to use every gift, resource, and opportunity to honor God and advance his kingdom. To do that effectively, we must recognize the impact of cultural encroachment—our lust for more and more things—and at every turn avoid being consumed by our sinful desires.

John's example of generosity extends to every area of his life, including his involvement in social justice and scores of compassion-focused ministries. He encourages people to give themselves first to Christ and then, as they are transformed by his Spirit, to give themselves wholeheartedly and unreservedly to help others. At Bethlehem, a culture of generosity is not the product of episodic events or building campaigns. Instead powerful teaching about the supremacy and glory of God continually evokes a response of love and loyalty to him, which is expressed in many ways, including generous giving.

For more than twenty years, John Piper has tried to instill a wartime mentality in his church members. He illustrates this by pointing to what life was like for many people during World War II. For those on the home front, many items were rationed, and people saved and donated what they had—things like rubber, metal, and nylon stockings—so that the soldiers on the front lines could have what they needed to fight effectively. Resources were deployed to those who were fighting and dying, and the rest of the population realized that they could contribute to this effort by saving and giving. In the same way, John believes, most people in churches today should try to cut back on their spending, "rationing their desires" so they have more to give to frontline, life-and-death ministries in their neighborhoods and around the world. Taking this idea one step further, Sam Crabtree has identified three categories of people in the war effort: those who go, those who stay behind and provide for them, and those who are disobedient and neither go nor provide as the Lord has directed.

Scott Anderson, the executive director of Bethlehem's Urban Initiative, again reinforces the motivation for these actions: "We don't give up things to earn points with God. We recognize the treasure in the field, and for joy over it, we sell everything to buy the field. In that sense, we aren't sacrificing at all, because we know that what we are doing has far more value than spending our resources on things that won't last." The satisfaction and joy that come from investing in the eternal far outweigh selfish pleasures.

The example of John Piper and the culture of generous giving at Bethlehem Baptist Church serve as a reminder that church leaders can have a profound impact on the level of generosity in their congregations. Your people will know if you have a problem with money or if you are living generously. We've seen some pastors who refuse to talk openly about money because they are struggling with poor financial habits in their personal lives. We have seen this enough times to know this is a pervasive issue that, left unaddressed, will undermine the mission and the fruitfulness of a local church.

Again, we want to say that we understand if this is an area of struggle for you. Being a pastor is usually not a lucrative career, and no pastor we've ever worked with decided to go into ministry to become rich. While many pastors make a generous salary, many others are just trying to make ends meet. Yet while we understand the challenges pastors face, we want to emphasize that it's not acceptable to allow your struggles to inhibit your ability to lead your church financially. You cannot skip teaching and preaching on this subject. Many pastors convince themselves that they can cover up their financial lives and keep this area hidden from others. Some become quite good at it, thinking that no one would ever guess that they aren't being generous with their money. But more often than not, we find that members will sense, at some level, when their pastor isn't fully committed to a life of biblical stewardship and kingdom generosity. Though they may not be aware of the full picture, they will tend to listen skeptically and unenthusiastically when the pastor talks about the subject of giving.

Don't Just Assume People Know

We find that people generally view church leaders somewhere between two perspectives. On the one side, some people are incredibly skeptical about pastors, their motives, and their lives. On the other side, there are some people who believe that a pastor's life is perfect. They expect their pastor to be free from worry, pain, and struggle. Regardless of where your congregation sees you on this spectrum, the people in the pew rarely have an entirely accurate picture of your life. They may have opportunities to see your family, your house, and your lifestyle, and, rightfully or wrongfully, they will assume certain things about you.

In our conversations with church leaders, we have learned that many of them feel that their weaknesses and struggles are unique to them. Often they are surprised to learn that nearly every pastor we talk to struggles with some of the very same issues and uncertainties. If you are a pastor or leader who struggles with financial integrity or generous giving, our intention is not to make you feel bad about yourself. It's unlikely that you would have picked up this book or read this far if you did not already have some desire to improve your personal money management and generosity leadership. We would simply suggest that the most significant step you can take right now is to confess to the Lord and perhaps your family where you are struggling, and let trusted colleagues and friends in your church family know that you haven't been leading them faithfully in this area. Though confession can be difficult and embarrassing, we have seen how God can use a pastor's candid acknowledgment of his struggle with financial management and transform it into a redemptive opportunity. What better way to testify that "we're in this together" than to stand before your people and admit that your personal money habits don't match the biblical precepts of stewardship?

Whether you choose to make such a confession privately or publicly, the immediate benefit is that acknowledging your struggle will free you from the burden of guilt and shame you've been carrying around. Your confession also will invite others, including many in your church family, to gather around you to affirm, support, and encourage you. We are convinced that what the Enemy wants to use to inhibit your impact, God will use for his glory. But this can happen only if you, as a leader, are self-aware enough to admit your shortcomings, and if you are bold enough to share your struggle with others.

Pastors Who Share

We have seen pastors who share with their people their own journey toward generosity see their congregations respond with a desire to follow suit. We recall in particular one pastor of a large suburban congregation. His income level was typical for a pastor, far from extravagant, and his children were just beginning to look at colleges — an additional expense. Yet he felt led by God to commit to giving away an additional 20 percent of his income for the next three years. Regardless of how much or how little money you make, 20 percent of your income is a significant amount! Taking into account that he was already giving away 12 percent of his income, this meant he was committing to give away 32 percent of his salary for three years. After hearing of his commitment, a wealthy individual made a decision to commit the largest single gift that church had ever received. When asked why, he said simply, "Pastor, I give because you give."

If you ever have been through a capital campaign (or as some refer to it, a strategic giving opportunity), you know that frequently the success or failure of the campaign comes down to the leadership phase, when the most committed members of the church make their commitment in front of the entire congregation, hoping to inspire the average person to move to a new level of generosity. As the leadership phase of a campaign builds, having a pastor share his own story of generosity can impact whether other leaders will follow. When a pastor talks freely about his personal struggle with money and invites others to join him on a journey toward generosity, we find that people aren't looking to stone him. Instead his story serves as an invitation to others to join him on the journey of becoming a generous person.

So if generosity is a struggle for you in your personal life, we invite you to consider using your position of influence to allow your own story of growing into a person of generosity to impact the habits of the people you lead. There are several reasons why we encourage pastors to take the lead in this area. First, there are certain things that only a pastor can say and do. Some people believe that only a pastor has the credibility to speak into their lives on such a sensitive subject. But the primary reason why pastors need to lead in this area is because Jesus led in this area, and the position of the pastor is representative of Christ's own leadership of the church. Because Jesus carefully and regularly revisited the conversation about the relationship between our faith and our money, pastors should do so as well.

We find that many pastors assume that their congregations already know what the Bible says about money, that people faithfully give the first 10 percent of their income to their church, and that members should be willing to give to the church and let the church decide how best to use the money. The reality we've discovered is that most people don't know what the Bible has to say about money, most don't have a concept of tithing or a habit of regular giving, and most members are frustrated by the idea of not having any input or say-so in how the funds of a church are used.

The assumption that church members know everything that the pastor thinks they should can cause confusion or lead to frustration. Wrong assumptions about where people are at in their journey toward generosity can end up eroding people's willingness to be generous and limit how open they are to following their pastor in this area. The truth is that pastors need to teach what the Bible has to say about financial resources *and* model that in their own lives and in the life of the church.

Partnering in Leadership

While we strongly encourage churches to hire a staff member dedicated to discipling and teaching on the subjects of stewardship and generosity, we do not mean to suggest that this position excuses the senior pastor from leading the church toward financial generosity. A senior pastor may be tempted to delegate these responsibilities to an associate, but these responsibilities are meant to complement the leadership of the senior pastor, not replace them. While a stewardship staff position can influence the congregation to give generously, only the pastor, as the church's "chief generosity officer," can effectively mobilize and inspire a broad base of support among the congregation. In our work with churches, some pastors have objected to this responsibility, reasoning that money is not a spiritual issue and arguing that it falls outside the jurisdiction of their work as a pastor. We couldn't disagree more! Not only is talking and teaching on money spiritual; it's a key responsibility of the pastor *as* the spiritual leader of his people. Humanly speaking, the pastor is the most prominent figure in any church. He is the primary spokesperson for the leadership of the church, and the one individual known by the broadest section of the membership. Since people give to those they know, like, and trust, a pastor has the most potential to develop generosity if he leverages his position and influence wisely.

Earlier in this chapter, we highlighted the story of Robert

Morris and Gateway Church. Robert and his stewardship pastor, Gunnar Johnson, do an excellent job of modeling the respective responsibilities of the senior pastor and the stewardship pastor. "Our senior pastor is a passionate guy about money management, giving, and generosity," says Gunnar. "We have seven people in our department, and we respond to the wake he is creating. He talks about money everywhere he goes, preaching all over the country, and he keeps us busy. He sets the pace. I was hired to build the ministry to support his vision. But we have like-minded hearts. He is blazing the trail, and I help create the mechanisms. He gets them excited, and I show them how to do it."

Now, you may not want or need a generosity team of seven in your church, but the key to a successful partnership between a senior pastor and a specialized staff member or team that champions stewardship is having clearly defined roles and responsibilities. We would suggest that some of the responsibilities should be shared among all the executive staff and frontline ministers of your church. Even better, a senior pastor should surround himself with a core group of committed givers who can help him navigate these waters successfully. Such a group should be part of a larger pastoral initiative to cultivate a culture of generosity within the church, rather than a onetime campaign to raise money.

Staff Giving

As a pastor, you should hold yourself, your staff, and your key leaders accountable for biblical stewardship and generosity. Many pastors choose to disregard this important work, but financial matters, whether of the staff or of a layperson, are always a pastoral issue. If staff members or leaders are contributing less, they will need care and counsel. If their giving has increased, someone needs to celebrate with them.

It is important that you seek to find a way of holding yourself accountable for becoming a more generous person. As we mentioned earlier, public confession can be a powerful catalyst as you move forward in your journey, but it is only the beginning. We also suggest that you find a group of trusted advisors who share your kingdom worldview and will challenge you to create more margin in your life in order to invest in the kingdom.

You may be inclined to take issue with our recommendation that you should hold your staff accountable for practicing generosity. We believe this is important, not simply as a matter of spiritual growth and accountability but also as a practical matter. In larger churches, it's common for the senior pastor to become insulated from the congregation and for frontline leaders to have more direct contact with members. If the senior pastor is practicing and promoting generosity but the staff and lay leaders are not supporting this vision, it's harder for the congregation to embrace it. Pastors need to hold their staff accountable for generosity if they want to communicate a consistent message to the congregation.

A staff member who is not financially generous may be struggling financially, struggling to accept the culture of the church, or a combination of both. Patience is needed to accommodate changes, but if time has passed and staff members aren't embracing the vision, you should not tolerate outright resistance. If a staff member refuses to be held accountable and resists the growth of a culture of generosity, then you as a pastor might need to see this as an opportunity to help that person find another church where they are better fit to serve. Though it can be difficult, a church can't afford to have a staff member on the fence, and a pastor who is all in won't tolerate anything less from the people who serve with him.

One of the churches we work with shared a story with us that illustrates the value of honest communication with your staff team. Their pastor noticed that a woman on his team, one of his key staff members, was not meeting the church's agreed-upon standard — that all staff should give at least 10 percent of their income to the church. Even though he was hesitant to confront this staff member, the pastor raised this issue privately and graciously with her. Through tears, she described how her husband, who was not on the church staff team, did not want them to tithe to the church, and she admitted that she felt conflicted about what to do. She was eager to give generously, but she also wanted to be on the same page as her husband about their finances. With her permission, the pastor was able to initiate a conversation with her husband and helped him to better understand the reason for the church policy about staff giving. This step of honest communication led to the husband and wife deciding to significantly increase their giving to the church and taking meaningful steps together on their journey toward generous living.

In addition to the staff and pastoral associates, there is one additional group you'll want to keep accountable: the lay leadership and key volunteers of the church. Depending on your church structure, this may include advisory councils, administrative bodies, ministry leaders such as deacons or elders, and even small group leaders. All of these people represent the church to those with whom the pastor might never or only occasionally interact. Our suggestion is that no one should fill a leadership role without some level of commitment to financial generosity. If you aren't careful in holding your leaders accountable, it will inevitably cause distractions and compete with the direction God is leading the church.

At the same time, keep in mind that many of your volunteer leadership teams will tend to be filled with people who are already faithful givers. In some cases, these individuals were raised in a culture of generosity and have never experienced a time when they decided to become generous. They may find it difficult to understand that generosity is a journey and that everyone begins at a difference place. As their pastor, you should encourage them to be patient with people who have not yet become committed to generosity and remind them that the goal is to move toward generosity from wherever one begins. Your church must learn to strike a balance here between the needs of your mature givers and the needs of those who are just getting started.

The Rich Young Ruler

The Gospels record the familiar encounter in which a rich young ruler came to Jesus, asking how he could secure eternal life. Jesus told him to sell everything, give the proceeds to the poor, and follow him. Because the rich young ruler failed to obey Jesus' instructions, he ended up walking away without the very thing he sought.

This passage is full of wisdom and can be applied in a variety of ways, but we'd like to offer one simple takeaway here: namely, that a pastor should invite his congregation to follow Jesus by taking defined steps toward a generous lifestyle. Jesus' command to the ruler is a call to each of us to leave behind our need to be in control and to follow our own plans for our money. The rich young ruler had his own ideas about how to achieve eternal life. He thought that he could obtain what he wanted within the safety of his personal wealth and his position of authority. But Jesus challenged the things this young man was trusting in, inviting him to leave all of that behind and simply follow.

Part of your responsibility as a leader is to model a lifestyle of financial generosity to your people. By doing this, you set the pace for spiritual growth and development in your staff, lay leadership, and larger congregation, who are invited to follow you as you seek to follow Christ. But you must also remember that generosity is never about what the church wants or what God wants from people. As Andy Stanley of North Point Church reminded us earlier, generosity is always about what God wants *for* people, not *from* them. God wants nothing less than for your congregation to join his mission in the world. You can trust that God has not only called you to guide your church to the place he is leading but also equipped you with the people and resources to get there—or at least to take the next step!

Key Ideas

- Generous churches are led by generous pastors.
- Congregations are not easily fooled; they can sense when their pastor struggles with money.
- Pastors must be transparent about their journey to generosity, knowing that people will respond gladly when they see that their pastor gives generously.
- As chief generosity officers, pastors have a responsibility to lead their church toward financial generosity and should never simply outsource that role to another staff member.
- Pastors should consider the view from the pew, because they risk forcing their perspective on the congregation, who might not yet understand giving and generosity.
- It's hard for people to ignore when a pastor says, "I'm all in."
- Pastors need to know what their staff is giving.
- Pastors have an immeasurable influence on their congregation.
- It is the job of leaders to assemble the resources needed to accomplish the mission.

Discussion Questions

1. How would you describe your personal journey of generosity?
2. When was the last time you told your congregation about your struggles or victories with money?
3. Do you monitor what your staff gives? Why or why not?
4. How do you ensure that your perspective on money is consistent with the challenges your members face every day?
5. How do you embrace your leadership role with respect to generosity? What new conviction can people hear in your voice when it comes to leading others in their personal habits and corporate responsibility?
6. In what ways do you take ownership of funding your church's ministry?

Chapter 5

LEVERAGE THE WEEKEND EXPERIENCE

Part of leadership is telling people what they don't want to hear. So many of you are afraid to talk about money. You are going to have to get over your insecurity about this issue of preaching on money. — *Rick Warren*

No event is more critical to the life of a church than the weekend experience. It is the place where the church gathers. In most churches, corporate worship is the most attended, most promoted, and most significant event. The vast majority of visitors, regular attenders, and marginal members will, at the very least, attend a weekend service.

We understand and respect the role that small groups and missional communities play in building community, teaching biblical living, and fostering spiritual growth, but we also recognize that, in many cases, only a minority of church members ever move beyond a weekend interaction with their church. Knowing this, a church's leadership must ensure that the weekend experience allows for transformation in the lives of those who attend. Rather than avoid or downplay the subject of generosity, church leaders must learn to speak on the subject when the broadest section of the membership is present and engaged in worship.

Various churches take different approaches to inviting people to participate in the weekly offering. And each church's invitation to give is usually consistent with its culture. Some churches are almost apologetic about having an offering, while others have removed it entirely from the service, replacing it with giving boxes in the gathering areas of the church. Still others, however, have found a way to incorporate it into the act of worship itself, emphasizing it as an essential part of loving and honoring God. "We've shifted away from the 'don't worry about the offering' mindset," says Clayton Smith, executive pastor of generosity at United Methodist Church of the Resurrection in Leawood, Kansas. "For us, the theology of that isn't right. We don't overemphasize or overask, but we do present it as a worship opportunity. If we apologize for asking for money, that only reinforces the stereotypes."

The Power of the Pulpit

Outside of a lecture hall, church is one of the few places where oratory and narrative shape the way an organization operates and the way people assimilate knowledge. The power of preaching should never be underestimated. We support the role of both preaching and teaching in the life of any faith community as an effective, people-shaping opportunity. Why do we emphasize this? Because if a church and its leaders want to create a culture of generosity, the pastors must not shy away from preaching on matters of financial generosity. Periodic sermons and regular teaching series on the subjects of finances, stewardship, and generosity ought to be delivered by the senior pastor. Again, we want to emphasize that while there might be other pastors on staff who are more comfortable speaking on these topics, and while there might be opportunities to invite a guest speaker during a special emphasis on giving, this not only can offend those who feel called to give but also can undermine the central leadership role the pastor plays in moving people down the path of spiritual formation.

We have seen, time after time, that churches blessed with an abundance of resources are led by pastors who are bold in their willingness to preach and teach about money. These pastors clearly articulate what the Bible says on the subject. This doesn't just mean that they regularly preach an entire series on money. Rather stewardship, money, and generosity are woven through many of their messages and will frequently make up the bulk of a message.

When a pastor uses his platform to spread the message of generosity in this manner, it may come back to him in unexpected ways. Consider the response to Rick Warren's 2009 explanation, reported on national news media, that the church was nearly $900,000 short on their budget. On December 29, Rick wrote a letter to his congregation and carefully explained that this was not because of poor money management on the part of the church staff but rather because of the great needs created by the recession.

THIS IS AN URGENT LETTER unlike any I've written in 30 years. Please read all of it and get back to me in the next 48 hours.

I have thrilling news to share with you below but first some seriously bad news: With 10 percent of our church family out of work due to the recession, our expenses in caring for our community in 2009 rose dramatically while our income stagnated. Still, with wise management, we've stayed close to our budget all year. Then ... this last weekend the bottom dropped out. On the last weekend of 2009, our total offerings were less than half of what we normally receive—leaving us $900,000 in the red for the year, unless you help make up the difference today and tomorrow.

Rick Warren appropriately used his role to explain what had been done and then asked the church to make up the difference. On Saturday evening, January 2, 2010, Rick announced that the people of Saddleback Church had responded with an outpouring of generosity, giving $2,400,000 in response to the appeal. As a result, the shortfall was erased and the church ended the year with a surplus of more than $1,500,000.

Contrary to what many pastors believe, people want to hear their pastor talk about money. They are eager to learn what the Bible has to say about money. They know that the world hasn't given them the full story. Many people crave an alternative approach to their relationship with money, and we believe it is the responsibility of the lead pastor to illuminate what a Christian perspective on finances looks like.

Tell Stories of Life Change

So how do you talk about money without becoming the church that *always* talks about money? To do this well, church leaders should consider the entire weekend experience, not just focus on the sermon. A worship service offers many opportunities to present stories of life change and to invite others to make changes in their own lives. This invitation can come through the chance to participate in the offering or to take part in some other special act of generosity. When *generosity* becomes just another word for increasing church funding, it will lose its ability to impact people's lives and to develop them as disciples of Jesus Christ. Instead we encourage teaching that shows how the act of generous giving frees the giver from attachment to the things of this world and demonstrates God's love to the receiver. Generosity, in this sense, is one of the most tangible, quantifiable ways that we experience God's power as revealed in the gospel.

The ultimate goal is to change lives. Connecting generosity with biblical teaching on life change reinforces the idea that people aren't being asked to give in order to fund budgets, buildings, or programs. It presents generosity instead as an act that nurtures the souls of both the giver and the receiver. Though you may encounter some criticism from individuals when you begin teaching on the subject of money, there is no greater response to your critics than to show them how these gifts are impacting people's lives. Whatever static a pastor might receive from talking about generosity and giving, it's worth it because of every life that is changed!

Home Field Advantage

Even though people attend church services less regularly today than in the past, the church still sees its people face-to-face more than any other entity in the nonprofit world. We call this "home field advantage." Hospitals, universities, relief agencies, and other nonprofit and charitable organizations would love to have the same opportunities to cast vision to potential donors that the average pastor has—and often takes for granted! While regular contact with members has always been important, it has become even more critical in the years since the recession started, because face-to-face interaction is key to developing and growing generosity in people. The global economic meltdown that began in 2008 reframed the rules about church giving, making it all the more necessary for the church to stand out from the rest of the nonprofit world.

So what should church leaders do with this home field advantage? We would suggest six practical things leaders can focus on.

1. *Build trust.* All charitable funding is given in an atmosphere of trust. Leverage the weekend worship experience by building trust in all you do.

2. *Cast (and recast) vision.* People have to be constantly reminded of the ministry vision of the church because vision leaks. There are three types of reminders—blast

(fire hose), soak (garden hose), drip (soaker hose). You can probably imagine what each of these would look like at your church. Keep in mind that there is an appropriate time for each. Use the blast sparingly, relying more on the soak and drip so that your people really absorb the vision and own it for themselves.

3. *Shape culture.* You may have great vision, but bad culture will cause problems in implementing it. As church consultant Sam Chand has said, "Toxic culture trumps vision." Culture is never neutral; it is either moving your ministry toward generosity or allowing you to drift away. Make sure you are always shaping culture so it is working for you. (See chapter 1 for a more detailed discussion.)

4. *Demonstrate impact.* Showing givers the results of their giving is like showing them a return on their investments—and people direct their charitable giving to where they see results. Numeric results will inspire some. Others will be inspired by stories of changed lives. No doubt, your church has stories to tell, but they may be hidden in the numbers. Make sure you are accurately reporting results and telling inspirational stories of life change.

5. *Enhance relationships.* People give to people, motivated by need and results. Build relationships with a broad spectrum of the people in your church in order to invite them to get involved. Make sure your schedule is not so full that you don't have time to connect with the people in your church who can help fund the vision.

6. *Highlight good stewardship.* Churches that practice good stewardship with the money given to them earn givers' respect. Look for obvious signs of waste or excess, and let your people know about key decisions you make to more efficiently use the funds entrusted to your church.

However you choose to get started, we want to emphasize again: don't ignore or underestimate the power and influence of home field advantage.

Your Worship Programming Strategy

To develop a culture of generosity, you must find ways to incorporate generosity into your worship programming strategy. Themes related to generosity should make it into the video production schedule, the worship set, and the announcements and should be part of the regular planning for the service. First-time visitors will describe your church by what they observe and experience in the service. And they notice everything, like what people wear, if someone was helpful, kind, or disarming. Did people bring coffee into the service? Were there some who used their smartphones to take notes? What kind of music was played and sung? All of these details create impressions for the visitor. They send a message about what kind of church you are. You can accelerate generosity in your church by paying attention to these details. What can you do to include the theme of generosity in the midst of the impressions they create? This will require careful thought and deliberate action.

The way you talk about money will also characterize the weekend experience. There are three elements to consider when you speak about money: frequency, language, and function. How often and when do you talk about money? When you do talk about it, what language do you use? And do your discussions of money demonstrate and highlight opportunities for developing generous habits?

If the only time you talk about money is when you need money, you aren't leveraging the worship service to create a generous church. There is a place for honest dialogue about the state of the church budget, but the all-too-common habit pastors have of speaking about finances only when the church is in need is unhealthy. As we suggested earlier, this is why it's important to regularly preach about generosity and stewardship as an essential aspect of discipleship and following Christ.

In addition, the language we use to speak about generosity and stewardship should not be burdened with a sense of obligation. This is not the place for motivation by guilt or shame. It is important that church leaders train themselves to speak about generosity as the only appropriate response to the grace of God. Far from an obligation, something we have to do, giving is something we get to do.

It's also important that you know your audience. Good communicators accommodate the listening habits of the hearer rather than their own personal preferences. In a given weekend, your church hosts hundreds of people with unique listening and learning styles. You must learn to design your message about generosity with many different people in mind. And consider ways to maximize other communication channels by providing supplemental materials such as pamphlets, books, or videos in a resource center, in the church lobby, or online.

Finally, when talking to your people about opportunities to exercise generosity, are you expressing the full range of possibilities? Again, the best way to do this is by telling inspiring stories. We have seen churches profile a family who takes their life savings and adopts a child from another country, or a business owner who does home improvement work at no charge for senior members of the community. Highlighting stories like these reshapes the way people think about generosity and inspires them to develop a "generous imagination" that gives them fresh ideas for how to practice generosity in their own lives.

Marketing experts believe that direct mail succeeds because it has a clear call to action. In fact, most direct-marketing professionals will tell you that you should always begin a campaign with two things: the offer and the call to action. If you aren't explicit in stating how someone will benefit from your product or service and you don't invite them to do something specific, then you've missed your opportunity.

We believe that this same principle applies when you invite people to take a step along the journey toward generosity. What are you offering? What benefit are you providing them? And what are you asking them to do right now? Churches that make an explicit appeal for people to move in a specific direction tend to engage a broader audience and get more people to respond to their requests. During the weekend experience, the offering time is an ideal moment for calling people to act. But there can be additional factors that subtly influence the congregation's participation. At what point in the service do you receive the offering? Is it merely jammed between two songs? Does it just sound like one of the many announcements that the pastor or the host of the service is pitching to the congregation? What is communicated prior to receiving the offering? How does this fit in with the elements before and after? Again, we want to encourage you to be intentional about how you use this time.

At Sun Valley Community Church, the weekly offering focuses on the church family's giving, but there are opportunities for visitors to participate as well. "When we are taking our general offerings, or even talking about a capital campaign, we tell visitors that this is the time for the church family to give, and we want them to feel no obligation," says lead pastor Scott Ridout. "Occasionally when we have special offerings, we'll do something like ask everyone to give the two smallest bills in their wallets, or the one largest bill. That's an opportunity for every person to get involved, and we tell them where their money is going. We did a smallest-bills appeal to help one of our members who was in the hospital. When people know who or what they are giving to, you avoid most problems."

Don't Just Give the Sermon on the Amount

To compete with the sophisticated messaging strategy of the traditional nonprofit world, churches will need to become more intentional and creative in how they talk about their budget, financial needs, and giving opportunities. Rarely is anyone moved by a black-and-white, line-item budget presentation.

And they are definitely not motivated by what we call the Sermon on the Amount. This is the sermon that the pastor preaches on money, stewardship, tithing, or some other related topic when there is a financial need in the church or it's time to take a special offering. One of the biggest mistakes that church leaders make in the area of preaching about generosity is that they raise the issue only when they are trying to raise money. When we consistently make this connection, we are training our people to tune out what God has to say about generosity. And we are saying that generosity is not about what we want *for* you; it's about what we want *from* you. We want our people to see that generosity and stewardship are part of the spiritual formation of every growing follower of Christ. So resist the temptation to preach about money only when the budget is tight or there is a need.

A good rule of thumb is that if you're not excited about preaching a message, no one is going to be excited to listen to it. When was the last time you preached a sermon before or during a strategic giving opportunity or during an annual stewardship emphasis that spurred spontaneous acts of generosity across a broad spectrum of your congregation? If that hasn't happened recently, it might be time to rethink your approach.

We know many pastors who preach using a series-based approach, deciding on a particular theme and expanding that idea over a number of weeks. In this model, it's easy to find a way of including the topic of generosity. However, remember that preaching on generosity should not be limited to a single series; it should be a consistent theme in the life of a church. Other pastors choose to schedule their preaching by following a predetermined preaching text plan such as the lectionary. If this is your approach, you may wonder how it is possible to creatively include the theme of generosity in your preaching. One of the best ways to do this is to emphasize the larger themes of the Bible. The core narrative of the Bible itself centers on the generous activity of God. It's the story of how God wanted to make sure we knew how much he loved us, how he did everything possible to ensure we could again be in a loving relationship with him. Once your eyes and ears are attuned to the core message of God's generosity in sending his Son, Jesus Christ, you will discover that you frequently encounter the theme of generosity as you work your way through the lectionary or through the Scriptures. You won't need to try to squeeze the idea in; it's already there, running through the pages of the Bible! The goal of our salvation is a generous life, and regardless of the text you preach, you can call your congregation to generosity by presenting them with the message of God's love and his gracious, generous work on our behalf.

Whatever approach you take to preaching, ask yourself three questions to help you pay closer attention to the message of the Scriptures. First, ask yourself, What does this passage teach us about God's generosity toward human beings? Second, ask, What can we learn about generosity from this text? And finally, ask, How should this inform our decision making so that we become less attached to the things of this world and more able to share with others? When a pastor is able to consistently draw out the gospel thread of generosity, it becomes less likely for people to associate the call to be generous with budgetary needs and requests for more funding. Instead it encourages people to grow in their understanding and practice of generosity as a core spiritual discipline of a Christ follower.

Consider Other Ways to Communicate

As we have suggested already, the church has no platform more persuasive than the pulpit, and the senior pastor is the authoritative voice that guides the church through contemplation and action. But there are also times when pastors should consider giving a platform to people who have allowed generosity to shape and transform their lives. A life of generosity becomes even more compelling when people see someone "like me" recounting how God has moved their heart and how their life has changed because of what they've learned. While the pastor bears the primary responsibility for communicating the message of generosity, not every idea or message about generosity has to come directly from him. In fact, having other people share their stories and insights might help to convince the skeptic who believes that any conversation a pastor has about money represents a conflict of interest, something done with selfish motives.

There may be times when you want to consider inviting a guest speaker who has knowledge of a specific aspect of generosity or who has an exceptional story to tell. We recommend that you do this sparingly, for there will always be the temptation to off-load the responsibility for preaching about money to someone else. Nevertheless, occasionally bringing in other voices can be effective and inspirational, especially when someone can share how an act of generosity has led to a changed life.

Finally, don't let the weekend experience be the only time when you distribute a message or series among the community. Use whatever technology is available to you to interact and dialogue with your members throughout the week and to empower them to share your message with their personal networks, ensuring that the conversation doesn't end when people leave the church campus. Incorporating technology into your overall generosity strategy can greatly extend the investment you're making to create a powerful, meaningful, and interactive weekend experience. Some pastors further connect with and speak to their congregation through regular video blogging. Others share information about life change during midweek e-newsletters. Established social media channels like Facebook and Twitter let people see how the pastor operates in everyday settings and add credibility to what he says in the pulpit each weekend.

Begin Where You Are

We rarely meet a pastor who feels that his current strategy is maximizing the weekend experience as an opportunity to create a culture of generosity. Some certainly are doing a tremendous job, but as for those who are new to the conversation and feeling overwhelmed, we want to make sure we don't lose you. Maybe you're pastoring a church as the only staff member, or maybe you're planting a church in an extremely poor neighborhood. Perhaps you'd like to focus on generosity, but you feel so loaded down with expectations that you're not sure how you'll squeeze it in.

Your interest in reading a book like this should be affirmation that you are moving in the right direction. Pray that God will open doors for your own generosity to grow and that he will provide ways for you to share with your family and your congregation what you're learning and experiencing. You'll be amazed at how your preaching and teaching will change as God shapes your thinking and living in light of generosity.

If we are to be people of the Word, we must be shaped by the words of Holy Scripture. One message in Scripture is very clear: we serve a generous God whose desire is for us to be generous with one another. We must shape our church cultures — and in particular, the weekend worship services — around this generosity. Anything less is closing the door on a corporate experience of the abundance of God's resources and blessing.

Key Ideas

- Leaders must connect conversations about money to stories of changed lives.
- A church needs to leverage three important platforms: the weekend experience, the church's website, and social networks.
- Churches have a home field advantage compared with other nonprofits, because they personally interact with members on a regular basis.
- Don't just give the Sermon on the Amount.
- Be honest with people when it comes to talking about money and church budget issues.
- Whether you preach series or follow the lectionary, the themes of generosity and stewardship can be found throughout the Bible because they are core to the Christian life.
- Despite what anyone feels, the pastor must talk about money.
- Give other people a platform to share their journey toward generosity.

Discussion Questions

1. When was the last time you preached a series on generosity?
2. How do you usually talk about money from the pulpit?
3. Are you reluctant to be honest with the church about issues related to budget and giving? Why or why not?
4. In what ways are you leveraging your position of influence to advance generosity in your church?
5. Describe a time when you allowed someone else to share their journey toward generosity. What impact did it have on your congregation?

Chapter 6

EMBRACE THE MINISTRY OF ASKING

Let us consider how we may spur one another on toward love and good deeds.
—*Hebrews 10:24*

If there is one thing that can make a pastor fidget in his chair, it is the thought of asking for money. Few pastors ever consider the key role that money and finances will play in their professional life when they sign up for a lifelong commitment to lead a local church. However unanticipated the task might be, it doesn't take long to realize that the role is unique to the pastor *and* essential to the work. Just as it is vital for pastors to call people to exercise their spiritual gifts in ministry, it is critical for them to call members of the body of Christ to invest their financial resources in the kingdom. And it is the ministry of the pastor to do the asking.

Sometimes the way we approach the connection between ministry and money makes people uncomfortable. We should view money not as a necessary evil to be reckoned with but as a partner for ministry. No ministry thrives without needed resources. If ministry is the vehicle for accomplishing our mission, financial resources are the fuel. Pastors who lead generous churches, who always seem to have abundant resources at their disposal, have had to come to terms with their apprehensions about money and ministry. Once they accept that the two are not polar opposites, they find freedom and confidence to lead their churches with clarity, care, and conviction.

We frequently hear people describe generosity as a particular kind of giving. For example, the theme of generosity is tied to everyday giving for the ministry operating budget or to a special giving opportunity such as a mission project or a building campaign. Sometimes generosity is discussed as a person considers leaving a planned gift as a legacy for future generations. We believe that generosity encompasses all of these, but it also goes beyond them.

In chapter 2, we talked about the importance of incorporating teaching on generosity into every part of your ministry. Talking about money should go beyond occasional needs-based appeals. It goes beyond learning fundraising strategies and techniques. While we can learn a lot from others in the nonprofit world, we must also remember that the church has a unique identity with a distinct time for gathering together and a specific mission and calling from God. Because these things are not often present in nonprofit ministries, these ministries are usually forced to rely on needs-based fundraising strategies and on direct-mail appeals. Churches, on the other hand, need to think about ministry and money in the context of discipleship, considering the broader implications of the Bible's teaching on money in the life of the believer and in the work the church has been called to carry out in the community and in the world.

You Have Not Because You Ask Not

Surprisingly, the biggest objection we hear from pastors who are uncomfortable talking about money or making requests before the congregation is that they don't want to be like "this" pastor or "that" pastor who they believe is only concerned about bigger buildings or their own financial reward. In response, we gently remind pastors that a focus on generosity does not have to be an "unholy shakedown" of the congregation. Your invitation to give is not supposed to be a ploy to get as much money as you can from your members. In fact, rather than being about money, a healthy pattern of teaching on generosity and bringing needs before the congregation creates a discipline that trains people in kingdom priorities. Giving generously helps us avoid becoming so attached to this world and its temporal kingdoms of power, influence, and authority that we end up forgetting our true purpose: building the eternal kingdom of God.

Leaders should pay attention to their own hang-ups, insecurities, or simple preferences because rejecting the ministry of asking, for any reason, will stunt the spiritual growth of your congregation and keep you from experiencing the rich blessings that God wants you and your church to experience. When we use others' poor leadership as an excuse to avoid God's call to live generously and inspire the people in our congregations to do the same, we fail to live up to what God expects of church leaders. As a pastor, you are responsible not only for your own spiritual disciplines but also for the way you teach others to pursue theirs.

You may not see yourself as a fundraiser. Good, because that's not what we are talking about. This is a ministry, the ministry of asking. And you can do it. You can learn to overcome any preconceived ideas about money and ministry that may have hindered you in the past, and you can overcome your uneasiness about the subject and call others into a culture of generosity. As a leader in the church, you must learn to ask, or you will forever be limited by your inability to move beyond the constraints of your own insecurities or preferences. Learning to embrace the ministry of asking is one of the keys to experiencing the abundance that God promises his people when they obediently follow him.

You may have noticed (particularly if you graduated from a college, university, or seminary) that most institutions of higher education have no problem asking for money. In fact, most have a large staff of people exclusively commissioned to do one thing: ask people to give money to the school. Why does a college invest so much in its development staff? Because the administrators know that asking is the most basic step toward receiving the funding that the college needs to accomplish its mission. What could happen, then, if churches adopted that same posture? What if the church and its leaders believed so deeply in their ministry to the world and knew so plainly that finances were necessary to continue that ministry that they began asking clearly and unapologetically—perhaps even audaciously—for the resources they need?

One pastor of a small church told us about the day he went to the mailbox, only to discover that one of his church members, who had recently deceased, had left the church $500,000. The pastor had no idea that a church of less than one hundred in attendance in a small town in Virginia would have a member with that kind of giving capacity. To put this in perspective, that gift was four times the church's operating budget for the year. Later the pastor learned that the large gift was only a small portion of the person's estate! He had never thought to ask, because he didn't realize that such giving capacity existed in his church. As a result, this giver may have missed out on the joy of giving this gift and others while living and able to see the impact of his giving.

Often, we evaluate the potential generosity of a person or family based on what they have given previously. In many cases, that level of giving does not reflect their true potential for generosity. In our conversations with hundreds of church members, it is clear to us that the church is missing a great opportunity. In many of these conversations, it's obvious that the church did not capture the heart of the giver because the pastor never took the time to ask.

The traditional nonprofit world knows this all too well, and they carefully work to build bridges to the people who sit in your pews. You have probably received requests for money from one of these organizations, some of them asking for significant gifts. Nonprofits often receive these large gifts, not because they are the best choice for people who want to give but simply because they asked and the church didn't. Think about how much money fails to reach the offering plate, instead going to other well-meaning organizations, all because the church simply fails to ask.

One of the churches we work with, a large, thriving mainline denominational church in a major metropolitan area, put this principle into practice in a recent capital funds initiative. The stewardship pastor took the lead in identifying financially blessed people who might be highly interested in what the church was trying to accomplish with the funds. He and the lead pastor presented the vision and the need to a small group of these people, who as a result pledged over half of the $10 million need. Many of these families pledged a much larger amount than they had ever given to the church. The catalyst behind all of this was the simple decision to embrace the ministry of asking.

It's What We Want *For* You, Not *From* You

The ministry of asking begins with a shift in perspective. Rather than thinking of stewardship primarily in terms of what a person can give to the church, we should understand, and help our members understand, that being generous is about following God, being a part of what he wants to do through people in his church with the resources he has given them. The difference between these two ways of thinking is subtle but significant. The first way of thinking is rooted in a concern for the needs of the church, while the second begins with the individual, their sense of calling, and invites them to share in what God is calling us to do together. Many pastors avoid talking about money because they fear it will make them appear selfish, both personally and professionally. Some take the risk because they know the church "needs" the gift. But when our primary focus is on leading people to respond to God's call in their lives, our view of generosity broadens and we are reminded that the body of Christ is not limited to a single geographic location or congregation of believers. It is a movement of Christ followers around the world who have joined God in bringing his kingdom to earth until Christ's return. Giving, with this perspective, is not a duty but an opportunity to respond to the grace of God. A Christ follower who has an appropriate understanding of grace will respond to support the work of God when he or she is asked to give.

You can learn the ministry of asking, which we believe can be broken down into three parts. We'd like to unpack each part for you, but first we want to emphasize the importance of an established, ongoing relationship with the person you are asking. In other words, make sure that you have permission to ask and that you know what to ask for. We'll talk more about this in chapter 7, but the basic principle at work here is this: people give to people. The more connection and respect the two of you share with one another, the more likely you are to be trusted and, ultimately, funded with a generous gift. Pastors who lead with an abundance of resources always make an effort to build relationships with the people who can fund the mission.

Prior to asking someone to give to the ministry of your church, you should take time to listen to his or her dreams and desires. We counsel pastors we work with to, whenever possible, meet one-on-one with a prospective giver, perhaps over coffee or lunch, simply to get to know him or her. We also suggest gathering small groups of key leaders who can share with each other their passions, heart, and desires. It's an amazing thing to watch people dream out loud. Sometimes the reason why we don't inspire key leaders in our congregations is because their dreams for the kingdom are larger than the picture we are painting for them!

Most pastors fail at asking for financial gifts because they have not spent any or enough time with the person they are asking. They fail to cultivate a relationship. That's when the ask becomes awkward and can even be offensive to the other person. We can say with certainty that pastors who are comfortable with the ministry of asking are not that way because they have the spiritual gift of asking. On the contrary, it's because they have spent time developing good relationships, making the request for money a natural part of their ministry in the lives of church members.

The Ask: Information, Inspiration, and Invitation

Any appeal for generosity consists of three parts: information, inspiration, and invitation. We have found that all three elements must be present in order for the ask to be effective and have the best chance of success. The absence of any one of these steps will likely hinder the process.

The first part of the ask is always *information*. You should be able to clearly articulate your ministry objectives, provide evidence of strategic planning, and outline expected outcomes. In many cases, the person you are asking is comfortable in leadership settings, may have occasion to analyze data, and can make strategic decisions. If she is a successful businessperson, she is probably not opposed to risk but is opposed to projects that have unclear objectives and are poorly planned. With enough clear, compelling information, she will begin to trust that your project is worth funding.

The second element of an effective ask is *inspiration*. After you have explained the details of the project and the vision behind it, you should draw connections to the giver's dreams and passions. For an ask to be mutually beneficial, your church's ministry must somehow help the giver achieve his goals, dreams, and desires. It's not enough for us to assume that the giver will give because we believe the project is important. It's imperative that you connect the project to the things that are most important to him. Otherwise you run the risk of making the person feel like an ATM. In other words, look for the intersection of the giver's passion and heart and your ministry vision.

The final element is the one most pastors neglect, the *invitation*. It does no good to give great information and to show how the church's vision is aligned with the giver's heart and then fail to provide a place for the giver to step in and offer a gift. There must be a moment of decision. Sounds familiar, right? We take for granted that as ministers of the gospel, we need to invite people to respond. Well, the ministry of asking requires an invitation too.

"You Can Do It. We Can Help."

We once heard Bob Buford, the founder of Leadership Network, explain to a group of pastors how Home Depot's famous tagline could help them understand the relationship between the one who asks for support and the one who gives it. All too often, the church says to someone, "We can do it. You can help." We, the church, have a plan to do some good in the kingdom, and all we need is the help, or financial support, of the church members. But this message thwarts your people's heartfelt generosity. A better approach is reflected in the Home Depot motto: "You can do it. We can help." What you, the giver, want to accomplish in God's name with the resources he has provided, we, the church, can help you achieve. This is not just a semantic difference. It's a completely different paradigm!

In many cases, the desire to give is already present in a person's heart, and there may already be some ministry that God is calling them to accomplish. Something that they uniquely care about. Generally, people walk into Home Depot with a purpose; they are trying to solve a problem, make something better, or build something new. When a person enters the store, he has some idea of the outcome he wants, even if he doesn't know the process to achieve it. At that point, an associate who specializes in that particular area and is familiar with the possibilities, hazards, and benefits of the project can become a guide for the customer, connecting his desired outcome with the process, tools, and knowledge to finish the job.

This same paradigm can be applied to the context of ministry. The giver, like the shopper, is looking for a particular outcome when she invests her charitable funds. The pastor serves as a guide to help her assemble the knowledge and other tools necessary to make her final decision. Still, the giver wants to feel that she is actively involved and in some cases driving the process. The church provides an avenue by which she can do that.

The potential for impact is multiplied further when we remember that we are merely facilitating the unleashing of God's resources to accomplish God's work. It's not really about us, as a church, at all; it's about what God is doing in this person's life and what God is calling them to do with the resources he has entrusted to them. More often than not, the dream God has for the person you are asking is larger than either you or they might have first thought.

Abundance or Scarcity

People tend to see the world in one of two ways: some believe that there are limited resources; others believe in an unlimited Source of resources. Those who have the scarcity mindset will never be able to reconcile their perspective with the ministry of asking. They will always believe they are in competition with everyone else for a limited amount of funds, and this limits their thinking and minimizes their impact. Because they fail to embrace the ministry of asking and have a limited view of God's abundance, they may never experience the joy of watching someone with a very modest income give a very generous gift to a building fund or mission project. They may miss out on seeing a family choose in faith to sell their home and move into a smaller house in order to use the proceeds to fund the kingdom.

Conversely, people who believe that God wants to amply provide are more enthusiastic about the ministry of asking. If we believe in a God without limits, we must accept that the resources we need in order to establish and grow his kingdom on earth are also unlimited. Yes, we must do the work of building relationships and inviting people to respond, but we also trust that the resources God has are plentiful and will support God's kingdom-building projects in our churches. When we think this way, we don't have to be intimidated when we ask for financial help. We know that God will faithfully provide what is needed for the work he wants to accomplish.

When you have an abundance mindset, you can even confidently encourage your congregation to give their money elsewhere, to other kingdom-oriented ministries and causes. And you won't panic when a giver in your church makes a large contribution to another charitable organization. You can encourage your members to grow in their understanding and practice of generosity, regardless of its destination. You can affirm generous behavior even when it doesn't directly benefit your church. You accomplish nothing when you criticize the decision of a church member who gives generously outside your church. His generous giving is a sign of spiritual growth and maturity. Embrace and celebrate that behavior with him. Your constant refrain should be, "As your pastor, I want you to be the most generous person you can become, for God's sake. If you think this is a ploy to raise money for our church, then let's talk about growing as a generous person by giving elsewhere." When we enthusiastically allow our people the freedom to give where God is leading them to give, we remove the suspicion that we are merely trying to raise money for our own purposes.

Living generously means living with our hands open. This way of living creates an inexplicable energy! Churches that experience an abundance of financial generosity have a kingdom vision and are excited to see God's work extending beyond their own congregations. And they are led by generous pastors who have embraced the ministry of asking.

Key Ideas

- Pastors fail if they raise the subject of money only when they need to raise money.
- The perspective is always what God wants for the congregation, not what the pastor wants from them.
- Resist the temptation to judge the generosity of a person based on what they have given previously.
- Before we can do any asking, there must be listening.
- A leader should connect a giver's passion and interest with the church's ministry.
- Asking people for money is helping them accomplish their dreams, not the pastor's.
- The ask always includes three things: information, inspiration, and invitation.
- The ministry of asking sometimes results in gifts that don't go to your church. Celebrate even when something is given elsewhere.
- The confidence to ask comes from a belief in an abundance of resources. Scarcity-minded people rarely ask.

Discussion Questions

1. Can you articulate your ministry plans clearly?
2. When you think about asking for money, what is the first thing that comes to mind? Is it a positive or negative feeling? Why? What impact has that had on your willingness to ask throughout your ministry?
3. What steps are you taking to ensure that you are listening for the needs and passions of various people in your church?
4. What percentage of your time do you, as a pastor, devote to the ministry of asking? What should it be?
5. Has a church member ever told you about a large gift he or she gave to someone other than your church? How did you react?

Chapter 7

DISCIPLE HIGH-CAPACITY GIVERS

It is easier for a camel to go through the eye of a needle than for someone who is rich to enter the kingdom of God.
—*Matthew 19:24*

The greatest opportunity to advance generosity in your church is the chance to unleash the full potential of the high-capacity people God has placed there. Our only fear in sharing this idea is that it is so simple and obvious that you might not recognize the great potential here. Financially blessed or high-capacity people are difference makers. Wherever they go, whatever they do, they make a difference with their leadership, their influence, and yes, their finances. In many cases, we see latent, powerful potential just waiting to be released, but more often than not these people are not being inspired to live up to that potential, and frequently they expect the church to make the first move.

Again, we want to emphasize that this is not a secret strategy for raising more money to fund your next project. Our suggestion that you begin discipling the most financially blessed people in your church is not a plan to get access to their money. Your heart must be set on reaching people because you see the difference their lives can make when they are unleashed to follow God and use the resources he has given them for his glory. Understanding the gift of giving and then calling it out in high-capacity givers is not without its challenges, but each challenge can be overcome with thoughtful planning. "There is often a dysfunctional relationship between the church and high-capacity givers," says Todd Harper, president of Generous Giving, a ministry that works with high-capacity givers. "There is plenty of blame to go around. The wealthy bring their own stuff to the party. Generally, in terms of first-generation wealth, people are used to being in charge, and that's part of the dark side. Their giving can have strings attached. People who have created wealth particularly do not embrace people controlling them. From a financial standpoint, churches try to do that. It's paternalistic — 'Let me tell you what we've got, see how you can buy in.'"

Todd suggests that churches should learn to approach the ministry of giving in much the same way they approach other ministries. Every church has a number of ministries that exist solely for the sake of ministry to people, not for anything they get in return. "From single moms to the homeless, ministries are designed without any expectation of receiving anything back," Todd says. "High-capacity givers are never related to that way. We always want something from them. As humans, we tend to forget that God is the provider. Instead we seek out who we can motivate and inspire to give money, rather than trusting that God will provide. There is always a quid pro quo — a transactional relationship. I'm struck by the fact that we are anxious to activate people's spiritual gifts, but in giving, it's with an agenda. We need to instead think about developing a person's gifts for the sake of the person and for the kingdom, not for our own gain.

"This is a spiritual calling—being spiritual directors to the wealthy," Todd continues. "At Generous Giving, we believe a pastor to this audience must have relational ability, be spiritually mature, be an influencer, be passionate about giving, be able to build trust, and be a self-starter. We believe these are nontransferable qualities."

The Church Vision

Discipling high-capacity givers begins with some homework. Start with the vision of your church. Is your vision clear and compelling enough to capture the potential these givers might have for the ministry of your church? Paint too small a vision, and the giver may miss the potential God has in mind for them. But paint too grandiose a vision, and you'll appear scattered and unrealistic. Neither impression is good. Many high-capacity givers are leaders of businesses or organizations. They've been successful. They know how to see what is possible, chart a course, overcome obstacles, and reach their goals. They understand that success begins by being clear about an organization's goals and how they will be achieved. "You have to remember that it's about vision and accounting for your actions," explains Todd Harper. "High-capacity givers think of themselves as stewards, and God has entrusted them to discern where they can prudently invest. They very much want to see a return on investment. Churches that do that—communicate vision and show accountability for the funds—experience success with these givers."

When was the last time you explored your church's core values? You can probably list them, but are you sure that the direction you're currently headed aligns with your stated values? If there is inconsistency—even a subtle shift—this group will pick up on it and want to know more. They will want to know, Are the core values of your church really shaping your leadership decisions? High-capacity givers see their financial capacity much the way an investor does. They need confidence that their investment today will yield a much greater "ministry return on investment" down the road. If they sense that the church isn't moving in a singular direction with purpose and mission, it will erode their confidence and willingness to unleash the giving potential God has given them.

The Pastor's Vision

After you've evaluated the church's vision, consider your vision as a pastor. High-capacity givers are used to sitting at the top, which can be a very lonely position, and they often empathize with pastors. They understand the pressure of making complicated decisions on behalf of the organization. These commonalities can become fertile ground for dialogue.

As a pastor, you should be able to clearly and passionately articulate your personal vision for a particular project and for the overall direction of the church. More than likely, the people you are talking with have earned their positions by making a number of good decisions, and they have learned by experience how to weigh risks and examine ideas carefully. High-capacity givers want to know that you have taken the time to process the opportunity with care and are concerned for the long-term sustainability of the church. Present the opportunity without hesitation and with a sense of confidence.

When a pastor struggles to define his vision simply and passionately, the opportunity becomes suspect or at least gets placed back in the pile "for further review." Always remember that there are many people and organizations appealing to these individuals. High-capacity givers want to make an impact, and many of them would prefer to support their home church. The tragedy is that they rarely get to hear the pastor's vision directly from the pastor, and more often than not, those who do are left wanting more.

Wealth Brings Complexity

Because of their apparent success, we tend to assume that high-capacity people don't need a lot of attention from the church. We forget that they too need to be discipled and guided in their growth as Christ followers. Even though they have been successful in certain endeavors, they have all the same problems as other families in the church. They may have relationship conflicts with their children and spouses, they may have addictions they fight against, and they may suffer from spiritual malnourishment.

In addition, they have a host of spiritual and relational challenges that are unique to them because of their affluence. Financially blessed people are often surrounded by attorneys, accountants, financial planners, and other professionals who help them protect and manage their personal matters. The more money a person has, the more likely they are to become a target for people who want something from them. Money doesn't solve relational problems, and it often creates an entirely new set of problems to deal with. Frequently, both wealthy people and their children don't know the motives and intentions of people seeking a relationship with them. Ironically, a life of great wealth can be a very isolating, lonely existence.

Jesus said it is easier for a camel to go through the eye of a needle than for a rich person to enter the kingdom of God. He singled out the wealthy as being at particularly high risk of missing the path to eternal life. As a pastor or church leader, this should be foremost in your mind. This is why it's important for the church to reach out to high-capacity men and women. They need to hear the gospel, and they need to grow spiritually—just like the rest of us.

It's important that the relationship you cultivate with high-capacity people is based on more than what they have to offer you. Don't become just another person representing just another organization that wants a payday. In fact, if your only intention is to ask for something, you are likely to fail. And by violating their trust in the church, you could also do significant spiritual harm. Your desire for relationship should be based on a genuine concern for their spiritual well-being, for their growth and development as followers of Christ. Your interest in them is not just a tactic or ploy; it's a natural outgrowth of the church's commitment to lovingly serve people.

Mike Miller, director of stewardship and generosity at NorthRidge Church in suburban Detroit, stresses the importance of relationships. "Before we think about the big things," Mike says, "we need to think about the little things — relationships. It's up to us to win the right to make the ask. At NorthRidge, our senior pastor, Brad Powell, understands this. He commits once a year to get twelve of our biggest donors together. Not to ask for anything; just to get them in the room. And God takes it from there."

Often, people with great wealth have great problems in their lives. And because many of the people they know want something from them, they often need a pastor more than they need a development officer or another great opportunity to give. Our encouragement to you is to seek out these difference makers, and when you find them, start by seeing them as people in need of a Savior. While their issues may look different from those of other members of the church, remember that even though wealthy people may appear to be on top of the world, we are all frail and wounded, in need of the grace and mercy of God.

Discipleship Is the Goal

To begin discipling the high-capacity givers in your church, start by creating environments in which you can build relationships with them. A dinner gathering or another low-key, informal outing might be a great way to start. Be careful that you don't allow the group to get too large. If you have many high-capacity givers in your church (and that's a good problem!), consider breaking up your meeting time into several smaller gatherings.

When you are together, let them see the ministry of the church through the eyes of the pastor. Use this time to cast vision and build trust. Be bold in sharing where you believe God is leading your church. Remember, the people you are discipling are used to the view from the leader's chair. Many of them sit there every day. More important, create opportunities for you to listen to them, and don't be afraid to ask for their advice, especially when embarking on a new initiative. Let them help you evaluate key moves before you make them. Often, this group can help you by asking revealing questions, allowing you to see the good, the bad, and the ugly concerning your new ideas. You may not always like what they say, and you may not always agree, but you will never regret listening.

Lincoln Berean Church began a discipleship process with some high-capacity people in this way. "Bryan Clark, our senior pastor, invited about fifteen of the area's leading businessmen to begin meeting monthly. These are top business owners and CEOs, not all of whom attend Lincoln, but people he knows," says Brad Brestel, stewardship pastor. "He's met with them over the last year. Not everyone is required to be a believer. No one had ever brought this group together before. Freeing their resources was not the goal; freeing them to follow Jesus was. He's invested in their lives."

While Bryan still joins the group at times, it's Brad who continues to develop relationships and disciple the group. "I am the stewardship pastor, but I am also an attorney with a finance background," Brad says, "and I meet with individuals about all kinds of things—legal issues, mortgage questions, debt consultations; it's really across the board. Some business owners have come in and want to know what I charge to take a look at what they're doing. I have probably had five to six couples, business owners, who have come to me and said, 'I love running the business, but I don't know how to manage resources. Will you help us?' That's been fun for me, because I become a strong influence toward

126 • Leadership Development

God in their life. Because I'm on the church staff, I can base it on spiritual values and bring everything back to the spiritual reasons to give and save, and help them discover how much is enough for saving and for investing in their lifestyle. It's good for us to wrestle through those questions together."

High-capacity givers know they have a unique opportunity to make a difference with the resources at their disposal. They likely already have some idea of what they'd like to do, but they also have some questions and need direction. Armed with information and advice, they will be the ones who make the final decision about who they want to support and at what level. We stress this because it is critical that we not confuse our role in the process. We are not spending someone else's money. We are simply providing them with the tools, advice, and opportunity to make an informed decision about how they want to steward God's resources.

Identify Opportunities, Not Needs

Generally, high-capacity givers want to give to opportunities rather than needs. They would rather invest in something that will grow than respond to an ongoing or immediate need. While there are always exceptions to this, we recommend that when interacting with high-capacity givers, look ahead instead of just focusing on the crisis situations that arise. Identifying opportunities will involve doing some research, setting a specific plan, and carefully setting goals. Because it's more complex to prepare and present an opportunity for investment than to present an urgent need, few pastors are able to fully realize the potential of high-capacity givers. Most pastors live in the details of the day-to-day ministry rather than getting ahead of the organization and charting a course for the future.

While we recognize that sometimes it's necessary to consider immediate needs when asking for gifts from high-capacity givers, we want to warn against playing the need card too often. In general, needs are reactive, repetitive, and degenerative. They provide little opportunity for growth. Because they are a reaction to something else, they rarely take on a life of their own and spur new development. Difference makers are most energized by discovering and evaluating opportunities for growth. So make it a point to identify and articulate these opportunities to your congregation.

Many times, high-capacity givers want to be a part of something only they can do, instead of simply funding the church's ongoing operational needs. That is why it's good to always have a list of key ministry initiatives that are not in your current budget. In other words, what ministry projects would you pursue if you had the funds? Look for opportunities to present these projects to the people in your church who are likely to have a passion for them. You will be surprised at how many of them get funded!

Different Perspective and Vocabulary

Conversations in churches often center on abstract or conceptual ideas. But it's problematic to assume that everyone is comfortable in the realm of the intangible. While successful people certainly can think this way, the reality is that many high-capacity givers are pragmatists. They want to know how you arrived at your conclusions, what you observed along the way, how you can replicate it, and what your plan is moving forward. When we approach a high-capacity giver without these details, we appear to them to be just another charity looking for money. Also keep in mind that many high-capacity givers have a completely different vocabulary than is common in the world of the church. They look at decisions through a different lens. They want details, they want access, and they want their voice to be heard in the process.

Access matters to most high-capacity givers. Often, they are part of the executive level of the companies they lead, or, if financially independent, they are used to being the one making the final decision. They expect to have access to or one-on-one time with the key leaders, including pastors. It's not that they are trying to buy their way into the pastor's office. Rather they believe that the size of their contribution of both money and expertise warrants deeper investigation on their part. In other words, they likely want access to the key leaders of the church because they want to be good, faithful stewards of the resources they have been given. When we deny them this access, we limit their ability to effectively invest those resources.

And we want to be perfectly clear that giving a high-capacity giver the opportunity to ask questions, hear our personal vision, and spend time with key leaders isn't evidence of favoritism; it is a sign of respect for who they are and the responsibility they bear in making decisions to best invest God's resources in the kingdom. Allowing financially blessed people in your church to explore ways to steward those resources in the kingdom is real, pastoral ministry. And so is caring for those in your church and community who are in need.

When difference makers feel empowered with details, with a voice in the decision, and with access to leaders, they begin the transition from a giver to an investor. Not many pastors are familiar with this transition or comfortable guiding it. The reality is that most seminary training simplifies teaching on stewardship and generosity by implying that church financial management consists of compelling people to give to the church and then letting the paid staff decide how to use that money. Unfortunately, when we adopt that posture and fail to communicate with our congregations—especially the segment that can make a significant difference in our financial trajectory—we end up losing the people who want to make long-term investments in our ministry. The church loses out on the gift that God intended to use to build his kingdom through your ministry, and the giver loses out on the blessing of giving and being obedient to God's call on his or her life.

Treat Difference Makers as Stakeholders

Difference makers in your church should be involved in key decisions, not because they have lots of money to give but because they already have a vested interest in seeing the ministry of the church flourish. In some cases, these individuals may be at the church long after the pastoral leaders have moved on to another church. Often, the greatest givers in a church are not people who have made one or two large gifts but rather those who have made a lifetime commitment to the church. They've witnessed the comings and goings of many leaders who have a vision from God. In some instances, "God's vision" for the church has changed with every pastor.

Take this into consideration as you develop your relationships with the high-capacity givers in your church. Think of yourself as their pastor and care for them as people. And never forget that it's not about what you can do; it's about what God can do through them.

Now, let's take this unique ministry to and with high-capacity givers in your church one step farther. What do you do when you've built a relationship, made the ask, received the funding, and the project turns out to be a failure? After all, it happens, right? Some ministry ideas just don't work the way we thought they would. Sometimes the ministry plan was flawed, and sometimes the plan was just poorly executed. Any pastor who has found himself in such a situation knows that embarrassment. And the thought of having to face the key people who funded the project can be overwhelming. Will they be upset? Will they leave the church? Will they ever trust me again? What will they say? Will they stop giving completely?

All of these questions are normal. Indeed, failure is normal. And you can be certain that the high-capacity givers in your church didn't become difference makers because they avoided all mistakes. In fact, they were probably bold enough to make enough mistakes to get it right. Every one of them has tried—with the best of intentions and efforts—to minimize the risk of new ventures. But the reason they call them ventures is because they contain an element of risk.

When risk is involved, failure sometimes occurs. It's really that simple. Successful people have a history of failure, and they will expect their church and pastor to fail from time to time. The most important thing you can do is learn from your failure.

Once, a pastor called us after what he thought would be a dreadful meeting with a high-capacity giver. The man had funded an outreach event that went horribly wrong and was not well attended. It was a disaster. Though the giver was present the night of the event, the pastor didn't have much interaction with him, worrying that the man would let him have it. But, fortunately, the story doesn't end there. The pastor eventually mustered up some courage and followed up with the man, and the giver was delighted to talk through the details of the event. He asked a lot of good questions that helped the pastor clarify what he could have done differently. Then the man committed to funding a similar event again if the pastor was up to it.

As the meeting drew to a close, the pastor couldn't stand it anymore—he had to know why this man was being so forgiving and understanding. The giver shared his belief that failure is the path to success. He had chosen to fund the project initially because he was pleased with the clear thinking the pastor displayed on the front end, and he was elated at the opportunity to share his insight with the pastor as they thought through how to do it again. This time perhaps with better results.

Our experience confirms that this is not an unusual response, but few pastors believe it until they've experienced it for themselves. The most proven way to protect the integrity of the relationship between the pastor and the high-capacity giver is to report the results individually, taking time to process them together, even when the event or project is a failure. Follow up often with the financially blessed people in your church who are investing God's resources in the ministry. Let them know what results their gifts are helping to make possible in the work of the church, in the community and in the kingdom.

Not about the Money but All about the Difference

We want to end this chapter by reminding you once again that the goal, in all of this, is not to give undue power or influence to people who give the most money. Pastors should approach wealthy givers with the goal of discipling them as followers of Jesus and equipping them to wisely steward resources so they can unleash the financial blessing God has given them to further the kingdom. Just as a church has prayer champions, children's ministry champions, Bible study champions, Sunday school or small group leader champions, God also provides giving champions who can help stretch thinking about generosity and the giving habits of a congregation. They help expand its capacity to share the gospel and make a meaningful, transformational difference in the local community.

Difference makers are aware of their wealth and their influence, but they want to do more than just give money away without any concern for how it is used. They want to make a difference with the money God has entrusted them with. They want to invest wisely, but in a different kind of portfolio, one that pays out eternal dividends.

Ken Williams, executive pastor at WoodsEdge Community Church, reminds us that a relationship with a giver in the church should always be a two-way conversation, not a one-way "sales pitch." Ken tells the story of a WoodsEdge member who owns a manufacturing company that employs a number of church members. As the local economy slowed, the man's business suffered. In talking with him, Ken learned that the owner was more concerned about how he would be able to continue paying his brothers and sisters in Christ than about his own paycheck. That added sense of responsibility only deepened his anxiety. In a sense, this member was already exercising his gift of generosity—and the church's most important task was helping him find peace with circumstances that were outside of his control.

A pastor may not be able to give the best advice on wealth management, but he does have spiritual authority within the local church and bears the responsibility for discipling the congregation—including those who are high-capacity givers with a heart of generosity. It takes time and effort to disciple people, but pastors must accept the call and work to complete it with passion and endurance. God has given you, as a pastor and spiritual leader, a unique ability and position to speak into the lives of these individuals. They will pay attention to what you say, how you live your life, the decisions you make, and the way you lead.

The truth is that the church needs wealthy people—and wealthy people need the church! It's not enough for us to limit our relationship with them to infrequent appeals when we need to fill the budget gap. It is not enough to make an ask for a large project. We must be committed to the spiritual growth and formation of every member of our congregation, including the wealthy member who struggles with perhaps the greatest temptation of all: trusting in his or her self-sufficiency rather than living in community with other believers, following Christ together on a common mission.

Key Ideas
- High-capacity givers represent powerful potential, but often they are waiting for the church to make the first move. Financially blessed people are among the most overlooked segments of a church's population.
- The financially blessed person has a confusing and complex problem. The good news is, they have a lot of money. The bad news is, they have a lot of money.
- Wealthy people are circumspect about the motives and intentions of almost everyone around them.
- Move into the circle of high-capacity givers because you want to disciple them, not because you need something.
- Financially blessed people see giving as an investment for future ministry returns, not just an opportunity to solve a problem.
- It's okay to report negative results; just demonstrate that you learned from the experience.
- For wealthy people, the interest is in the difference they can make, not the money they can give.
- Let financially blessed people interact with one another. Put them together in community, and they will impact each other.

Discussion Questions
1. Do you know who the high-capacity givers are in your congregation?
2. What was the subject of the last conversation you had with a member of this group?
3. Have you ever gathered small groups of high-capacity givers together to share passions, hopes, and desires surrounding the ministry of your church? What was the result?
4. How can you begin to build trust—and keep it—with your high-capacity givers?

5. What tools, advice, and opportunities are you providing for your high-capacity givers so they can make informed decisions?
6. Are you currently discipling any financially blessed people? Who do you need to reach out to in this way?
7. What aspects of your church's vision have been shaped by the conversations and interactions you've had with high-capacity givers?

PART 3

IMPACT

Chapter 8

MEASURE PROGRESS

No one has ever become poor by giving.

—Anne Frank

One of the tried-and-true tenets of leadership is this: you can't manage what you don't understand, and you can't understand what you don't measure. For many years, stewardship in the church was relatively informal, based largely on the honor system. Members brought their offering envelopes completed with all the essential record-keeping information. Churches then compiled and reported the total numbers to the congregation. Denominationally affiliated churches registered with a local or national office that amassed the data, did some minimal analysis, and reported back to the churches.

In this chapter, we want to suggest some ways to develop a level of financial measurement that moves beyond simple record-keeping. The data you collect has the potential to reveal undiscovered ministry opportunities for your church. Changes in giving patterns almost always represent an opportunity for ministry, and we believe it is critical that churches use the power that comes from tracking giving to observe these changes and uncover these opportunities.

As church leaders, we are given responsibility for the churches we lead, including their financial management. Pastors must learn to take ownership of the church's financial administration in order to develop trust and confidence, two key ingredients for creating a culture of generosity. We have found that a leader's sense of ownership is greatly aided when he can track and analyze the congregation's giving habits and the church's use of money.

After all, you can't manage what you don't measure.

Show Me the Data, Tell Me a Story

In the years since the recession began, a new type of giver has emerged. This giver is empowered with information and access to the key leaders of the organizations and causes he chooses to support. If the church is to attract the interest of generous givers, it must learn to become more financially transparent and open than it has been in the past. Traditionally, the default approach to giving was that people would give to God and let the leadership decide how best to use the money. But in this new, empowered paradigm, the giver wants to know how his money is being invested and what results it is producing. In other words, givers want to know if the money they give is having a measurable impact in the kingdom.

Tradition has also taught—particularly in smaller churches—that distributing a line-item copy of the church budget will satisfy the curiosity of any church member with questions. In reality, few people know how to read operational reports or budgets. Many families don't even have a personal budget. So how can we expect people to glean insights into the church's ministry investments from such a sterile financial report?

Even though presenting data can be challenging and may require a creative approach, data is precisely what the giver needs to affirm that his investment in your church is making a difference. Like it or not, many churches must now compete with very focused nonprofits that want to present their own ministry goals and needs in order to win the minds and dollars of people in your church. We aren't suggesting that it's wrong for people to give gifts to a nonprofit instead of the church. Rather we want to encourage giving to both, with the church being the primary destination. All too often, however, when people choose to give to a nonprofit instead of the church, it's because the church has failed to present a compelling picture of its vision and finances.

Rather than promoting the easy data dump, churches should take a different approach by repackaging that data into story form. We are made in God's image, and we are emotional beings. Even the most rational, stoic person often makes decisions that aren't based purely on empirical evidence. Giving is both a rational and an emotional process, so we should honor that reality as we talk about money and ministry.

Storytelling is a powerful tool. The ancients knew this. And much of the ancient history we have in written form today began as oral tradition. A viable alternative, or supplement, to presenting a traditional budget is telling stories of life-changing impact. When it's time to promote an event, describe the life change that occurred at last year's event. When it's time to talk about money, show a video, invite personal testimonies, or simply retell the stories of how lives were changed in recent months. And remember that this kind of storytelling can happen outside of the face-to-face conversation or church service, through the creative use of technology and social media, which enable us to tell these stories twenty-four hours per day, seven days a week.

Churches that have developed a mature culture of generosity are excellent storytellers. And the stories they tell not only affirm the decision of the individual giver to support the church financially but also empower people to spread that story within their own spheres of influence. Often, when a church empowers the individual giver this way, the church ends up receiving sizable gifts from nonmembers or even nonattenders because these people are moved by the church's impact and participation in expanding the kingdom.

ROI is a common business term meaning "return on investment," which describes the result of an initial investment. It can be positive or negative, but ultimately the goal of any investment is to create more value for the investor.

We have adapted the ROI for the church by creating what we call the mROI—the ministry return on investment. If we can picture the givers in our church as investors or shareholders in the work of ministry, this helps us understand their need to see evidence that their gifts are making a difference. When we clearly demonstrate an mROI, we build confidence because we show people that we've done exactly what we said we were going to do. This confidence building is critical to encouraging people to give future gifts and to making the ask for large gifts when the time comes.

Obviously, no church member expects a dividend check for their investment in a particular church ministry. But they do expect to hear that their investment has accomplished something that they can't do on their own, something that affirms the things they are deeply passionate about. Remember the Home Depot slogan? "You can do it. We can help." The more effectively we measure the impact we make, the more clarity we can have when we report back and share the ministry return on investment.

Which Benchmarks Matter

Some of the churches we've worked with are preoccupied with benchmark studies on stewardship and giving. They want to know how their church compares with the national averages on per capita (or per household) giving. And they are preoccupied with overarching trends across the world of philanthropy. Sometimes church leaders ask us these questions because they don't know what else to ask. We believe they mistakenly assume that meeting or exceeding the national averages for giving is the ultimate goal.

But the problem with a national average is twofold: first, it is national in scale, and second, it is an average. Because we all do ministry in a particular locale, our issues are always unique to our context. It can be discouraging or flat-out useless for churches to compare their giving with that of a congregation on the other side of the country. A church in Montana shouldn't compare itself with a church in Beverly Hills. Because both churches are included in the national average, you may get some interesting numbers to think about, but nothing that you'd want to live and die by. And a church plant made up predominately of young families or students shouldn't compare its giving with that of an established church full of the movers and shakers in a large city. Benchmark studies can inform our thinking on certain subjects, such as health care costs and compensation. But giving is an entirely different issue, and these studies generally are not appropriate for comparison. Instead of comparing ourselves with other churches, we should measure ourselves against ourselves.

Consider how retail chains use benchmarks. When they want to evaluate their health, they don't track their sales across the board—the total sales of all their stores. This muddies the data because it includes both same-store sales and new-store sales. Instead they consider the same-store sales, which are the records of existing stores and their performance over time. If a chain has a consistent trend in growth in same-store sales, then it is generally considered successful and sustainable.

We believe that the same approach is helpful when analyzing the giving trends in a church. Rather than measuring itself against other churches, a church should measure itself against itself over a period of time. In other words, a church could track the growth or decline of giving per household over the past twelve or twenty-four months. Or it could evaluate the percentage of attenders who make a regular financial contribution. Data like this will reveal the truth about the church's specific habits rather than how the church compares with external norms. Growth in the number of households that give, in the average gift size, and in the number of large gifts are positive indicators of a culture of generosity. On the other hand, a significant decrease in these key areas is a sign that something isn't right and may be inhibiting the generosity of the people.

Another very useful exercise for churches to complete is a demographic study that reveals the household income of the neighborhoods near the church. If a church has multiple sites, it is helpful to break this down by campus location to get a more accurate picture of each location's giving potential. The data for such a study, which is publically available and generally comes from census figures, can provide insightful information such as average household income. This will provide a church leadership team with a rough standard by which to calculate the giving potential of a congregation. To calculate the giving potential of a particular zip code, multiply that area's average household income by 1 percent or 5 percent or 10 percent. The result is a giving potential range: what is possible for the average household in your congregation to give to the church, ranging from 1 to 10 percent of its income.

To determine the actual average giving in your church, divide the total annual giving by the number of households in your church. You may have to estimate this based on average attendance. You can now compare what your congregation gave with what it has the potential to give. Almost every church that does this exercise discovers that their congregation is giving about 2.8 percent of the average household income in their area. Theoretically, then, the potential for giving in most churches is around four times larger than the current giving. Assuming that your church is like most others, if your total giving is $250,000, your potential is $1 million. If your total giving is currently $10 million, your potential is probably more like $40 million.

Conducting this exercise is a great reminder to church leaders that people usually are not giving at their maximum capacity. It also reminds you that what is possible is much greater than what you see today. Many church leaders assume that because *they* are giving generously, everyone — even wealthy people in the congregation — are also giving to their maximum capacity. But this simply isn't true. This exercise won't enable you to predict next year's giving, but it can begin the conversation about how to move closer to your potential for giving. People responsible for growing a business can attest to the importance of knowing your potential, because it shapes your strategy, determines the level of risk at which you are willing to operate, and creates a hunger for greater capacity. All of these things are crucial in maintaining a focused effort on developing a culture of generosity in your church.

Fellowship Bible Church in Brentwood, Tennessee, was one of the first churches we saw pursue what has since become known as the One Percent Challenge. The leaders at Fellowship determined that if everyone would just give 1 percent more than they had been giving, the impact wouldn't just be incremental; it would be exponential! If every giver in the church gave just 1 percent more, the leaders were convinced, the church would never have to ask for money to fund special mission projects, to cover budget shortfalls, or even to build new buildings. And the results of this simple strategy were stunning. Over the next few years, average giving per family grew to 6.4 percent, and the church paid down more than $3 million in debt, funded a $1.1 million campus project, and increased giving for global outreach by $1.5 million.

Another church took a similar approach and created a video that illustrated what would have been different if church members had raised or lowered their giving by one percentage point in the previous year. The message was very clear: a 1 percent drop in giving would have significantly limited the ministry potential and would have made it impossible for the church to have done some of the most exciting ministry they had accomplished in the previous year. However, church members saw that the opposite was also true: had they given just 1 percent more, the increase in ministry capacity would have been profound.

Pastors Should Know

As pastors decide how to participate in building a culture of generosity, they often wrestle with whether they should be privy to information about how much people give to the church. James 2:1–4 is often used as an escape clause that gives the pastor permission to be ignorant of people's particular giving habits: "My brothers and sisters, believers in our glorious Lord Jesus Christ must not show favoritism. Suppose a man comes into your meeting wearing a gold ring and fine clothes, and a poor man in filthy old clothes also comes in. If you show special attention to the man wearing fine clothes and say, 'Here's a good seat for you,' but say to the poor man, 'You stand there' or 'Sit on the floor by my feet,' have you not discriminated among yourselves and become judges with evil thoughts?"

Some leaders interpret this passage to suggest that we should avoid knowing who is rich or poor and how much people in our churches are giving. They believe that knowing these things will lead to discrimination and favoritism. We have had numerous leaders tell us with pride that they don't know what people give—and never want to know! Hearing this makes us wonder what a trip to the doctor would be like if doctors weren't privy to details about our health. How would a doctor know how to treat us, what medicine to prescribe, and even what goal to have in mind, without knowing the state of our health? How effective would a coach be if he never noticed the needs or potential of his team or paid attention to the stats of the individuals he wants to recruit?

What if a teacher never looked at the grades of his students to determine who needed extra attention and who was catching on quickly?

We expect doctors to know specific information about our health condition. We expect coaches to recruit players who meet the team's greatest needs. We expect teachers to grade papers and monitor the learning of their students. Yet when it comes to spiritual formation in the discipline of giving, we don't want to know where people are at? In our opinion, this attitude makes no sense, yet many pastors vigorously continue to defend it. In some cases, the pastor may want to know this information so that he can appropriately care for and disciple the people in the church, but the trustees or bylaws of the church prevent him from doing so.

This secrecy of giving can be crippling to a church. We believe that monitoring giving information increases the leadership ability of the pastor in the following areas.

- Encouraging staff in their giving to the church
- Developing high-capacity givers
- Evaluating church leaders for financial leadership
- Identifying spiritual issues (changes in giving, up or down, almost always require a pastoral response)

If you accept, as we have suggested, that the pastor is ultimately responsible for shepherding the spiritual health and long-term sustainability of the local church, then it is *essential* for the pastor to know how much people are giving. One of the most concrete expressions of spiritual growth or decline in a person's life is not what a person says, how busy they are with church activities, or how many boards or committees they sit on but how they are stewarding the financial resources God has entrusted to them. Jesus reminds us in Matthew 6:21, "Where your treasure is, there your heart will be also." Our giving reveals the true priorities of our hearts. As a church leader, if you want to create a culture of generosity in your church, you will have to find a way to stay informed about the giving habits of your people.

Giving Is Personal, Not Private

The James 2 passage we highlighted a few paragraphs ago rightly raises the issue of playing favorites within a body of believers, based on their financial capacity. At the time the epistle was written, many Jews believed that people who were materially successful in life had been blessed by God and that those who weren't successful had been cursed by God. Since many of the early Christians were steeped in this tradition, they also tended to favor people with means.

James warns against this tendency, and we couldn't agree more! Knowing what people give, however, is not the same as showing favoritism to them. As a leader in the body of Christ, you may need to wrestle with the temptation that comes from knowing the details of what people give, but ministry leaders must deal with this temptation in a mature way rather than avoiding this information altogether.

Sadly, some pastors do let their knowledge of a person's generosity influence their conduct toward that person. But on the whole, we find that pastors are able to hold this knowledge carefully—as they would other types of private information—and they are able to use it to nurture spiritual growth in the people they love and serve.

We believe it is far more dangerous not to know what people are giving. Why? Because it's impossible to help people take steps to grow in the spiritual discipline of giving if we don't know their habits. This is true both for the person who has little financially and for the person who has much. Giving is personal but not private. Pastors should know what people give and be able to track any variances in giving. We tell pastors that every change in giving is a pastoral issue and should be followed up on appropriately.

For example, a first-time gift is typically an indicator of spiritual commitment. A large, onetime gift is often a sign of a spiritual response. Faithful giving that increases over time is a sign of someone committed to his or her faith and to your church. Don't you want to know what God is doing in each of the lives reflected here? Of course you do! That's why it's essential to have accurate information.

Recently we talked with a pastor who had noticed a significant decrease in giving from a church member who had been a faithful giver for many years. It seemed strange to him, so the pastor called the man and asked him to lunch, not to talk about money but to better understand what was going on in the man's life. In just minutes, the member explained that he had decided to retire but was having a difficult time making the adjustment. He was a quiet man who would never have approached anyone at the church to share this difficulty and seek support. Had the pastor not known about the man's giving habits, or had he left the issue untouched, the man might have left the church out of shame or embarrassment, and the pastor never would have known about this opportunity for spiritual growth.

In general, the people in your church who don't want you to know what they give are the ones who are giving little, if they give anything at all. People who do give may even want you to know, because they want to celebrate with you as they exercise their spiritual gifts and practice the discipline of giving. They want to share the joy of doing life together and working cooperatively to fund the kingdom-calling God has given your church.

One final note: Now that you've read this chapter, you might be nervous, wondering how to put all of this into practice. Objective data collection and research may not be part of your skill set. We would encourage you to find several committed laypeople in your church who have run businesses or have been successful in personal investing. Often, these individuals are glad to share what they've learned and to find a volunteer opportunity that fits their area of expertise. Let these people serve as a support group as you craft the skills you need and learn to ask the right questions. You don't have to have an MBA or become a financial guru in order to be successful at measuring the giving habits of your members, but providing this kind of leadership is the responsible thing for the shepherd of a local church to do.

Your willingness to move in this direction will not only reveal the giving potential and habits of your church but also help you gauge your progress in creating a more generous culture. And from time to time, it will lead you right into the midst of unexpected ministry opportunities.

Key Ideas

- Measure progress by showing the data and telling the story.
- A change in giving is a pastoral issue.
- You can't manage what you don't understand. You don't understand what you don't measure.
- You must demonstrate mROI.
- Temptation to show favoritism is not an excuse to not know what the people in your church give.
- Giving is personal but not private.
- It is more helpful to measure your church against itself, using previous years' financial information, than to measure against national averages.
- Measure so you can forecast what is next and what is possible.

Discussion Questions

1. How do you currently measure the giving in your church?
2. Who is responsible for interpreting the data?
3. What is your staff policy regarding who has access to information about the giving habits of your congregation? How might that policy need to be changed?
4. Most churches have a strategy for helping people with debt. What is your strategy for helping people with wealth?
5. Do you spend a lot of time comparing your church's performance with national benchmarks, or are you comparing your data with your church's own previous giving habits?
6. How is information about your church's giving utilized in ministry decisions, budget planning, and forecasting?

Chapter 9

YOU ACCELERATE WHAT YOU CELEBRATE

I have found that among its other benefits, giving liberates the soul of the giver. —*Maya Angelou*

Everyone enjoys a celebration. The work that must be done prior to finishing a project or meeting a goal may not be all that fun, but we push through the hardships and the challenges because we know that there is a reward at the end of the day. It doesn't matter if you're an ultramarathon runner who completes a fifty-mile race or a baby boomer completing his first 5K; that experience of crossing the finish line and running toward a crowd of people who've been waiting for you is worth the work and the struggle. The joy of celebrating at the end provides us with the strength we need to push through those moments when we feel like we aren't going to make it, when we're ready to give up.

We've all experienced the strain of difficult times, when you have no other option but to stay focused, push through, and keep putting one foot in front of the other. The ability to do this is what separates people who talk about doing great things from those who do them. And as you consider what it will take to create a culture of generosity in your church, you may feel overwhelmed and wonder where to begin. Please know that you aren't meant to run this race alone. Not only is it more exciting to share this journey with others, but you may even find that you can exceed your own expectations with the support of people who encourage and challenge you.

We have seen that churches that create a celebratory atmosphere around the practice of generosity have a much higher percentage of people who are aware of and engaged in the conversation. If we believe that being generous is a joy and a privilege — something we get to do and not something we ought to do — then it makes sense to celebrate whenever we have the opportunity to give.

In his regular *Encourager* e-newsletter, directing pastor Charles Anderson of University United Methodist Church in San Antonio, Texas, perfectly captures this spirit of celebration. His letter is personal and powerful, and it connects people's giving to the church's larger vision.

> As I write this letter to you on the afternoon of March 10, I can only praise God and thank you for what has happened in our church during the last four weeks.
>
> Just four Sundays ago, at the conclusion of our first-ever Global Impact Celebration, you stepped forward and volunteered just under $308,000 in Faith Promises for the remainder of 2009 — an amount equivalent to nearly 5 percent of this year's Operating Budget. Families and individuals of all ages and stages dedicated themselves to second-mile giving to causes beyond the walls of this church. Simply amazing and totally inspiring.
>
> Then, in worship on March 1, our church officers clearly set out the challenge of retaining our church staff during a time of national financial contraction. Our personnel and finance leaders asked you to pray and seek God's guidance. They set a deadline of today — March 10 — for your action.

This afternoon, March 10, the Finance Office reported the following:

New/increased pledges: $151,945.00
Cash collected: $187,318.51
Total: $339,263.51

Way to go, church!

Our Finance Director, Debbie Vignes, wrote to me: "Truly amazing. Never before have I seen Christ working so powerfully in lives of the members in this congregation. It is indescribable the humbleness I have felt in listening to the conversations with many members this week.

"We've had a UTSA college student giving from her college fund, because of what this church has done for her.

"We've had a 10-year-old give $11.25 — every dime she has — in response.

"We've heard miracle stories of anonymous gifts, land transactions, business deals, and estate settlements miraculously coming through for folks, empowering them to give special gifts at this special time."

Way to go, church! Do you realize that, in a time of economic upheaval that's unprecedented for most people, you have come up with nearly *$647,000.00* in new ministry resources in one month? Just think of the people that you have affected — not only the staff people and missionaries whose jobs you have preserved but also the countless people they will reach for Jesus. Truly, this past month has confirmed everything good, right, and true that I knew and thought about this congregation. God is good ... all the time, and especially right now!

Celebration Changes Expectations

What you choose to celebrate most often in your church will eventually become what is most valued by your church. Celebrating generosity in the life of your congregation reminds people that God is transforming hearts, minds, and lives through the investment of their resources. Pastor Bob Coy of Calvary Chapel in Fort Lauderdale, Florida, believes that intentional congregational celebration challenges leaders and members to change their attitudes about giving from a minimalist, 10 percent approach to a wholehearted surrender of all we possess. He offers four insights.

1. By celebrating the cause of Christ, we place our priorities with his kingdom rather than with our personal gain.
2. By celebrating integrity in finances, we keep ourselves from abusing resources.
3. By celebrating generosity, the church comes together to see what giving does for the kingdom, enjoying the privilege of obedience together.
4. Finally, by celebrating frugality, we set aside as many resources as we can for God's work, storing up our treasure in God's work rather than in personal gain.

American culture affirms and celebrates certain decisions, choices, and behaviors. For example, being physically fit, accumulating wealth, and rising to positions of power and influence are applauded, and most people—consciously or not—want to achieve those things in their own lives.

Positive reinforcement can be used to shape the expectations of our congregations as well. When we celebrate certain behaviors, we reinforce the notion that these are good and desirable things for people to pursue and strive to develop in their lives. When a church honors people who have a deep commitment to pray, others may recommit their spiritual lives to a deeper understanding and practice of prayer. When we affirm people who have read the entire Bible, it's likely that a group of others will commit to doing likewise. We've seen the same effect with the practice of generosity. When we acknowledge and celebrate the giving and generous habits of people, others see that such behavior is something good, something they want to emulate.

Consider how Rick Warren announced the response of Saddleback Church to his 2009 year-end appeal that we mentioned in a previous chapter. At one of their Saturday evening services, Warren let the church know that $2.4 million had been raised after his letter was posted on the church's website. "This is pretty amazing," Warren told his congregation. "I don't think any church has gotten a cash offering like that off a letter." Warren creatively made the announcement by bringing out twenty-four volunteers, each holding a sign that read, "$100,000." He made it clear that the total amount had come from members—not outside groups or individuals—and that most of the donations had been under one hundred dollars.

Using positive reinforcement should not be construed as peer pressure or an attempt to manipulate people into doing something they don't want to do. It is more like the idea of encouraging "one another on toward love and good deeds" (Heb. 10:24). Also, keep in mind that the behavior we are trying to hold up and promote is not negative or harmful to the individual. On the contrary, giving generously is evidence of God's work in a person's life. When we celebrate generosity, we are celebrating the goodness and grace of God, and we are prayerfully expecting that the contagious spirit of generosity will spread within our congregations.

Other Kinds of Celebration

We don't think it's odd to celebrate baptisms, baby dedications or christenings, salvation experiences, calls to vocational ministry, or calls to lay ministry positions such as deacons, trustees, or elders. Many church traditions have even established rituals and ceremonies around each of these. And we expect these familiar celebrations to be part of our church life. We would think it strange to skip a baby dedication or christening for fear of offending someone.

Yet when it comes to giving, many churches do exactly that: they avoid celebration. They may do this out of fear that affirming some people might make others uncomfortable. Or they may fear that affirming givers will tempt them to become prideful or self-righteous. So many churches avoid acknowledging and praising acts of generosity. We must learn to resist this, because it is right and good to acknowledge obedience to God in the area of our finances and to acknowledge and celebrate the amazing work God is doing in this area of a person's life.

We realize that for most people, money and faith come with a lot of baggage. But what if our avoidance of the issue is part of the problem? We would suggest that many of the negative attitudes that people have about money and the church might stem from one central issue: the failure of the church community to celebrate and acknowledge God's work in this area. Instead of openly celebrating generosity, churches often choose to value financial secrecy. Or, on the other extreme, they reward people who give the most money with positions of influence and authority. Churches have developed all sorts of unhealthy, unbalanced habits. Some applaud new faith commitments but don't treasure spiritual growth; some celebrate programming milestones instead of ministry effectiveness. When we celebrate the wrong things, it leads to unhealthy behavior and eventually creates an unhealthy culture. That's why we must be careful in this area, especially as it relates to money. If we fail to celebrate generosity in a healthy, balanced way, we shouldn't be surprised that our people don't value it.

Celebrating stories of changed lives assures us that our investments of time, money, and talent are not in vain. In many church traditions, the corporate worship experience offers two critical moments for celebrating life change. The first moment is baptism. Throughout Christian history, baptism has been a time when the community makes commitments to the one being baptized and when a new believer may be given the opportunity to make commitments to the community. Baptism and its accompanying commitments emphasize the importance of our common faith, the determination to practice the faith within the community, and the celebration of new life in Christ. Baptism is certainly one of the most significant visual representations of a changed life. It should be a participatory time of celebration, not, as it is in some churches, just another item in the order of worship. Churches that celebrate life change often make a big deal about baptisms. They plan events around it. They preach about it. They talk about it. Like Christians throughout history, they recognize the power of baptism in the life of individual believers and in the life of the church.

But there is another moment that regularly occurs in the life of most churches and in the worship service, one that also has the potential to showcase life change: the offering. The Old Testament repeatedly teaches us that bringing offerings before the Lord is a spiritual practice—a vibrant, visible way of celebrating the Lord's goodness. Sadly, in most churches today, the offering has become so habitual that the leaders no longer give much thought to it. Though they may not say so, they are demonstrating that the offering is not as spiritually important as the music, the sermon, and the time of prayer. In some cases, because it often falls near the end of the service, some people miss the offering time altogether because they leave early to beat the crowd out of the parking lot. In doing so, they miss the chance to respond to the blessings of God and to participate fully in the life and work of the church.

It should come as no surprise that churches with an active, vibrant culture of generosity are intentional about the role and the function of the offering in their worship gatherings. How are you utilizing your offering time as a means of spiritual formation? One of the best ways to do this is by using the offering time to celebrate changed lives and spiritual growth. Sharing stories and emphasizing the offering as a response to God's goodness can captivate imaginations and shape hearts in ways that lead to generous giving.

Taking Givers for Granted

It is sad but true that many churches take their givers for granted. Most nonprofits, on the other hand, understand just how difficult it is to find prospects, cultivate them, and see them become givers. They take great pains to identify these people, to build relationships, and to maintain those relationships. Frequently, churches expect that people simply will give and that it is not the responsibility of the church to acknowledge or express appreciation for the gift. Not only is this just plain rude to the giver; it may lead the church to feel entitled to the monetary gifts. This can grow into an unhealthy attitude that turns off generous individuals and families.

Churches must learn to be generous in their expression of thanksgiving for the generous gifts they receive. Churches that experience abundance in their funding execute a strategy of thanking, one that nurtures their relationship with givers. Very few churches have a strategy of thanking. They have neither a plan in place nor a sense of urgency to execute that plan. Instead they think, "Since people are giving to God, why should the church be responsible for expressing thanks when it's a private, spiritual matter? Why should we say thanks to some people when we can't possibly say thanks to everyone?" It's important to wrestle through these questions. You are not the first one to ask them, nor is yours the first church to consider how it might implement a strategy of thanking.

It is essential to build a system that will ensure that gift acknowledgements and thank-yous aren't overlooked. Most church leaders intuitively know that this is a good idea, but they have no idea where to start. Traditional nonprofits know the value of saying thank you and have learned that people who are thanked are more willing to give a second gift shortly after giving the first one. This is why a gift to a smart nonprofit organization or cause is typically followed up with an immediate response that includes an appeal for a subsequent gift. We're not suggesting that churches copy this approach. This is not about getting more out of your people. It is about inspiring generosity. You'll have to decide how your church can best practice thanking its givers. But countless individuals have given incredible amounts of money to the church over the years, and many of them tell us that they would love to receive a thank-you every now and then. They admit that they usually don't give to receive a thank-you. Most often, they just want to know that someone noticed the gift and affirmed the desire that led them to give in the first place: wanting to make a difference by serving the Lord with their resources.

Every successful strategy of thanking takes into account first-time givers, an increase in giving habits, and special gifts. When we pay attention to and acknowledge gifts only during certain seasons of the year, we minimize the ministry opportunity that can be found in an individual's giving trends. Even small increases in giving deserve acknowledgment. When someone gives to your church for the first time, you should celebrate this important step. Giving is an external expression of an internal commitment. Therefore when someone gives to your church, he is confirming that he has connected and is ready to move to deeper levels of commitment and engagement with the community.

In general, when someone gives to your church, it is a sign of commitment. When a person writes a check, gives a gift online, or fills out her name and address on an envelope, she is sending a strong signal to the church. It is, in all likelihood, not her first time attending. The giver could choose to remain nameless and faceless, but instead she has taken steps to make sure the church knows that the gift has been given. This gift is a big deal, especially in a tough economic climate, and the only appropriate response is to acknowledge that step of faith and thank her for her gift. This can be done with a phone call, in person, or even with a handwritten note. Many churches use a variety of responses to ensure a scalable approach to follow-up.

A thank-you note to a first-time giver can be one of the very first personal points of contact between a pastor and an attender. The note can simply say thank you for taking this important step of faith, thank you for trusting the leadership of the church to use this money wisely. This kind of encouragement can inspire the giver to take the next steps he needs to take on his spiritual journey. And that's pastoral ministry.

Although many nonprofits use this thank-you as an opportunity to ask for another gift, we encourage churches not to do that. Instead your approach should be very simple, thoughtful, direct, and personal. Remember, your purpose in doing this is not fundraising. You are celebrating the giver's spiritual growth through giving. You accelerate what you celebrate.

As you develop a strategy for thanking, you should also consider special gifts. From time to time, someone will make a large gift to the church. The amount is not the issue; the issue is that the giver has given what for him or her is a special gift. This may be in response to a capital initiative or mission effort. Other times, people are so moved by God that they make a special gift out of a compelling desire to make an impact in the kingdom.

When someone makes a special gift, you or your staff should make it a priority to reach out to this individual or family, and if it is a very large gift, we suggest that this be a personal, one-on-one discussion. It is essential that you, as a pastor, understand what prompted the gift. Ask the question, "What is the Lord doing in your life that has caused you to give such a generous gift?" And then listen for the answer. This is vital, in order to encourage and celebrate the life change expressed in the gift and also to understand what part of the ministry he or she is connecting with. This allows the leader to affirm the frontline ministry staff of that particular area and to encourage other frontline ministers to operate with the same strategic emphasis.

Many times, people who give large gifts don't want to be named publicly. Unlike traditional philanthropists, a church giver doesn't usually expect to have his name affixed to a building, etched into a plaque, or even mentioned in a newsletter. Care must be taken to keep the special gift in confidence. However, just because the giver's identity is kept confidential from the congregation doesn't mean that the giver doesn't want to talk privately about why he made the gift and what God is doing in his life. The worst thing we can do is to ignore this person and miss the opportunity to celebrate the spiritual growth in his life.

Effectiveness versus Faithfulness

As you begin to celebrate the developing generosity habits of your members, it's also important to understand the difference between effectiveness and faithfulness. We believe it's best to hold these two in tension with one another. Effectiveness is about results, benchmarks, and making an impact. When we say a gift is effective, we celebrate the impact that was made, not merely that the gift was given. Relaying a gift's potential effectiveness is an important component of the ask, and it frames how we celebrate with people who have committed to being generous givers.

Faithfulness, however, is different. It involves exhibiting the same behavior, in the same way, consistently over a long period of time. Faithfulness is clearly a godly quality, and every church must learn to show appreciation to faithful givers. But being faithful doesn't necessarily mean that a person is growing. In fact, the greatest temptation of faithfulness is plateauing. In other words, you could be faithfully stuck, never changing year after year. If the goal is spiritual growth, then we must create a dynamic culture of generosity that encourages members to move to the next step of engagement, purpose, and sacrifice.

Instead of focusing on either effectiveness or faithfulness, we should develop our strategy of celebration around both: being faithfully effective. Our moments of celebration should seek to connect the growth of the giver to the increased impact their giving has produced. As we focus on effectiveness and making an impact, we should track and report the results. No one wants to see their gift intended for one thing be used differently without purpose or explanation. Every giver — no matter the size of the gift — wants to know that their generosity made a difference.

Don't Be Afraid to Share the News!

In 2008, we worked with a church that was making its annual appeal for its benevolence fund — a single, year-end offering that would pay for all of the benevolence needs of the church for the entire budget year. The recession had hit many members of this community hard. Many professionals who attended had lost their high-profile, high-paying jobs, leaving them in a financial crunch. In making the appeal, the leaders of the church emphasized that they were aware that people were struggling financially and might not be able to participate. But they also acknowledged that some were doing well, and they presented the congregation with an opportunity to help those who were struggling. When we asked about the response to the offering in early 2009, we learned that the church had received the largest year-end benevolence offering in its history — but the leaders had never shared this with the congregation! We were surprised to hear that, and we asked them why. They didn't have a clear answer for us; they could only cite a vague concern that the church might think that too much money had been designated for the special fund. We respectfully disagreed and urged them to share with the larger body what had happened.

When the leaders reported the results of the congregation's generosity, the church erupted in celebration, something the leaders had not at all anticipated. Members were proud to be part of a church that focused on caring for those in need, which included helping people stay in their homes. This turned out to be an incredible opportunity to share in the joy of generosity, and it had taken only a few minutes to tell the story of the congregation's generous behavior! What a loss it would have been to miss out on that churchwide celebration.

Churches that celebrate the generous giving of their members will accelerate the practice of generous living. The net result will be spiritual growth in concrete, transformational ways — ways that can be explained only through the work of the Holy Spirit. When we celebrate generosity, we are reminded that the source of all things is God, and we gain a front-row seat to his work in people's lives.

Key Ideas

- Catch your people doing something good. People expect the church to point out where they are doing something wrong.
- What you celebrate changes your culture.
- Don't underestimate the impact that can come from having a strategy of thanking.
- Churches are notorious for taking their donors for granted.
- Make it a big deal when people give to your church for the first time.
- Monitor the giving habits of your members. Significant variances are signs of spiritual turmoil and spiritual growth.
- Be intentional and strategic in the way you take the offering.
- Celebrate generosity at least as much as you celebrate attendance, baptism, and other special times in the life of the church.
- Instead of arguing the merits of effectiveness versus those of faithfulness, concentrate on both — to encourage your people to be faithfully effective.
- When you make an ask and your people respond, report the results and celebrate!

Discussion Questions

1. When was the last time you made a big deal about the first time someone gave to your church?
2. What happened when you visited with someone after noticing a major change in their giving? Did you discover an unspoken, hidden ministry opportunity?
3. Why is it easy for churches to celebrate faith decisions and event participation but not generosity?
4. What happens when your church celebrates the wrong things?
5. Is it possible that you're taking the generosity of your congregation for granted?

Chapter 10

GENEROSITY IS THE NEW EVANGELISM

Let us not be satisfied with just giving money. Money is not enough, money can be got, but they need your hearts to love them. So, spread your love everywhere you go.
—*Mother Teresa*

This is a book about generosity, not a book about fundraising. We've said that a number of times. We work with churches not simply to help them fund budgets or meet campaign goals—although those things may result from implementing the practices in this book. But if that is all we're going to achieve, we will have missed something along the way. We work with churches because we believe that following Jesus means learning how to follow him in every area of our lives, including how we handle our money.

The truth is that God doesn't need our money but knows that our orientation toward money reflects our obedience to the lordship of Christ and how well we grasp that he is the source of all we have. As followers of Christ, our goal in life is not gaining power, possession, or prestige for ourselves. We exist, along with the entire body of Christ, to fulfill the Great Commission until Christ's return. Generosity offers one of the most powerful ways for us to leverage the blessings of God for the advancement of the kingdom. Best of all, when the church acts with generosity to serve others, it is a clear picture of Christ, who at the cross generously gave his life and all he had so that we might find life forever.

Financial hardship has a way of breaking down the walls that separate us, even in the church. The sudden loss of wealth and security reminds people that our net worth on paper—our value in the eyes of the world—can change at any moment. During the last recession, people started to question what really matters in life and began to think about what is of lasting value. Individuals who had placed their hope in the markets began to recognize that paper is really nothing more than paper; it has no lasting value. Two people who before may have been separated by the divide between poverty and luxury now found themselves in the same pew, seeking answers to the same questions: Where are you, God? What is your plan for me?

Unfortunately, history shows us that the insights we gain in these moments of clarity, when the divisions created by money evaporate long enough to reveal what is truly valuable and how much we have in common with one another, become obscured again all too soon. How can we prevent that from happening as our world moves toward economic recovery? How can we learn to retain the insights from the lean years when the years of plenty return?

As we mentioned at the beginning, we don't believe that money is inherently evil. Yet we do believe that money should play a less significant role than it currently does in the lives of most Christians. A follower of Christ should be guided by the direction of the Holy Spirit rather than the highs and lows of the Dow Jones Industrial Average or the NASDAQ. Economic downturns remind us that as believers, we all have similar balance sheets. None of us stand before God with anything to offer him, and we are all dependent on the same mercy and gift of grace that he offers us in Jesus.

Conversations about money aren't going away. As leaders in the church, we must learn to recognize that everyone is talking about money—both the person across the street and the person in the pew. The real question is this: How will you and your church use this opportunity—the interest that people have in money, and their desire to talk about it—as a way of connecting them with Jesus? The growing movement of generosity and financial stewardship among Christians presents a compelling alternative to the silence many churches have maintained in the past on the subject of money and its relationship to faith. So how will you respond to the questions? How will you engage the conversation?

Common Ground and a Common Experience

Since 2008, churches have witnessed large numbers of people flocking to seminars and workshops about debt and financial planning. Programs that previously struggled to attract interest have filled up. Financial classes have become popular with people in the church and in the community.

It's important to recognize that while our doctrinal beliefs give us unity as followers of Christ, we are also bound together by common experience. It is often our common experience that provides us with the solace of a human connection. There is something about our ability to help an individual in need that sparks a light in our eyes and opens the person's heart to the message we have to share. When we choose to be generous with what we have, we find ourselves locking arms with people in need. The growing emphasis on sharing what we have and giving generously of our resources to others is quickly becoming one of the best evangelistic efforts in America today.

The church has a unique message for times of economic uncertainty. Jesus provides us with an alternative approach to money, an approach that celebrates the sharing of our resources with one another. What we are describing is not an economic model that forces people to share their resources with each other, nor is it a political agenda. We believe that the church must begin to challenge Christians to behave in ways that are consistent with what they profess. Why? Because the world—the lost people all around us—is watching and paying attention to how we respond in times of trial and testing. Jesus reminds us in Matthew 5:14, "You are the light of the world. A town built on a hill cannot be hidden." When we act in ways that are consistent with our commitment to Christ, a watching world notices. We cannot hide who we really are, and generosity reveals that our faith is genuine and true.

All too often, however, we wait for people to come to us, raise their hands, fill out a response card, or walk down an aisle to make a profession of faith before we set them on a path of spiritual formation. What if, instead of waiting for people to come to us, we began to see everything in life as part of God's formation of our souls? Not only is generosity an expression of our faith in Christ; it can also be a formative experience, even for people who have not yet come to faith in Christ. Inviting someone who has not yet decided to follow Christ to participate in an act of generosity can create an atmosphere of life change, a positive receptivity to God's Spirit. Too often we assume that this can happen only in a worship service or through a sermon or small group study. But nothing is more powerful than inviting someone to participate in changing someone else's life. Experiences have the power to shape our lives, transforming the way we see and approach the world around us. Encouraging others toward generosity may be the most fruitful evangelistic exercise your church will ever undertake.

As we live before a watching world, skeptics and cynics will find it nearly impossible to find fault with genuine acts of generosity that demonstrate that our hearts have been set free from our love of money and things. When we give for the benefit of the kingdom, to serve others in love without expecting anything in return, people get something worth talking about. Far from being a stumbling block, money can be a connecting bridge to people outside the church.

When, as a pastor, you begin to incorporate generosity into a strategy for reaching others with the message of God's love, you start moving your members into partnership with people beyond the walls of your church. Generosity highlights the potential a church has to bring people together, regardless of whether they have any vested interest in the church itself. If people truly care about serving others and having an impact, they want to be involved, even if they don't want to directly support your church. For example, we have worked with a very large, traditional church that every year takes a special offering that it uses for charitable investments around the city. This fund supports a mobile dental office that treats impoverished children, and it pays for improvements and beautification efforts for buildings like hospitals and public schools. Some of the people who financially support this effort would never identify with the church or call themselves Christians. Yet this partnership with the church puts them in contact with believers who can both show and tell them the good news of the gospel.

The Great Commandment Meets the Great Commission

As we think about all that the Bible has to say about generosity, two moments in the New Testament stand out to us. The first is the Great Commandment, when Jesus instructs his followers to love God and to love people. The second is Christ's order to his followers to go and make disciples. This is the Great Commission. When our faith shapes our money habits, we are affirming our love for God and our obedience to him. But we must also allow our faith to influence the way we love the people around us. Our faith in God compels us to go and make disciples. What if we began calling our people to use the resources God has given them in order to make a difference in the lives of those around them—lost neighbors, coworkers, and friends who do not yet know the love of God?

We all know that the two highest-attended Sundays for churches are Easter and Christmas. What if, instead of simply trying to draw visitors on these days, churches announced that they were going to give their resources away to serve the community? Community Christian Church, located just outside of Chicago, is one of the leaders in the church generosity movement. Both in their personal lives and in the life of the church, pastors Dave and Jon Ferguson have thoughtfully created a culture of generosity. Each year they host something they call the Big Give. During this weekend, all the money collected is given away to a short list of selected ministries that serve the community. In other words, this church has made a conscious decision to operate on fifty-one weeks' worth of offerings, not fifty-two. This weekend is so full of vision and celebration that members of Community Christian invite their friends and neighbors to the experience so they can witness firsthand the hundreds of thousands of dollars that are given away—all in a single weekend. Many of these guests get their very first exposure to Community Christian at this incredible event. Because the congregation is so inspired by this idea, the offering for this weekend is usually two or three times the church's normal weekly offering. Over the years, the congregation has learned to expect the Big Give, and it is one of the highest-attended—if not the highest-attended—weekend events of the year. This is a sign that generosity has become a core value of the church. The Big Give is evidence that the church is doing something different to impact the city of Chicago, and people who need to hear the gospel are confronted with that evidence as a sign that God cares about them too.

Another church that is modeling this kind of generosity is Cross Timbers Church. In 2011, the church made the decision to give away its entire Easter offering. At Cross Timbers, Easter is one of the two days of the year when the church has the most visitors; presumably a number of them are looking for a relationship with God. Knowing that visitors and people seeking God would be at the Easter service, Cross Timbers chose to give away what is often one of the largest offerings of the year. They did it to make a statement about their values and beliefs as a church. An unbelieving world can debate a lot of things about the church, but generosity like this sends an unmistakable message.

We want to challenge your church to consider having a generosity weekend as part of its outreach strategy. Whether you decide to give away a certain amount or to operate on fifty or fifty-one weeks' worth of income for a year and give away the rest, we urge you to do something radical and remarkable. You may decide to support a variety of international charitable organizations, to put the money toward local mission efforts, or to distribute the funds within your congregation by inviting people who have needs to come forward during the worship service.

Advertise in the community, telling people what you're going to do. Encourage the congregation to invite their friends and neighbors. You could pass out invitation cards or use video they can share via social networks to maximize the exposure. Then be sure to capture the service on video as it unfolds. Just consider what would happen if your church's generosity prevented a family from losing its home to foreclosure, helped a single mom feed her kids, or helped a recovering addict pay for a treatment program. Do this not to prove how great your church is but to highlight the great God we serve. Your actions, like light shining in darkness, draw attention to God's love by meeting the real needs of real people.

The generosity movement has played a pivotal role in helping evangelical churches rediscover the balance between proclaiming the gospel and promoting social justice. This is especially true among church members who are part of the millennial generation (a.k.a. generation Y, next generation, or echo boomers), who tend to be activists rather than traditional churchgoers. An activist is someone who is not comfortable with the status quo. She wants to make fundamental changes to the current state of affairs. After repeated attempts to find a way to work within the system, she may eventually break away and work outside the system to challenge and reform it. This is what is taking place today as many churches break away from traditional ministry practices and adopt a new way of doing things that leads to measurable impact and changed lives. The millennials aren't satisfied with three points and a poem; they crave something more hands-on. If the church does not provide this for them, they will look elsewhere to other well-meaning organizations who may not share the belief that it is God alone who can transform a person or a community.

Gain the World, Lose Your Soul

Jesus once asked, "What good is it for someone to gain the whole world, yet forfeit their soul?" (Mark 8:36). The practice of generosity is God's gift to us; it helps us resist the snare of consumption and the idol of greed. The lure of wealth and possessions can consume us, and the best way to fight our own lusts and desires is to pursue a lifestyle of generosity. If Jesus is Lord, then we must learn that all that we have, are, and ever will become is a gift from God. This means we are responsible for sharing with the world the gifts we are given. This idea is central to the Great Commission. By helping people follow the Great Commandment, loving God with all of their heart, soul, mind, and strength, we learn to love others with divine generosity. The mission of the church is to call people to love God and others, something that is possible only through the grace of God given to us in Jesus Christ. Spiritual formation that emphasizes generosity and the giving of what we have for the sake of others honors Jesus' call to mission and to making disciples.

The church will be irrelevant to the world if we fail to practically live out what Christ has done for us. If what we say, read, and pray does not result in love for others, then we have missed God's intention, and our lives will fail to bear fruit for the kingdom. Nothing demonstrates the authentic spiritual growth of a believer more compellingly than spontaneous acts of generosity, welling up from a heart changed by the grace of God.

Corporately, a pastor can emphasize the importance of generosity whenever he talks about the mission of the church to reach the world. If all you talk about are programs and expenses when you teach on the subject of generosity, you are missing the point. The goal of cultivating generosity in the hearts of your people is not to pay your staff, build a bigger building, plan more programs, or execute your next event. The goal of giving generously is the spiritual formation of people so they are prepared and mobilized for ministry. Ministry to others is the visible fruit of faith, God's way of helping us to establish a connection with other human beings and ultimately bring them to an encounter with his life-giving grace. Generosity is the place where the Great Commandment meets the Great Commission!

For those of you who find it a stretch to see generosity as an outreach strategy, we encourage you to find a church that has experimented with radical acts of generosity. Ask how this has changed the culture of the church and what life change has occurred as a result. We once met with a church that was sitting on eighteen months' worth of operating expenses in reserves and was complaining about not being able to make necessary improvements to the nursery area. They had experienced a baby boom in their church and knew they either had to renovate their space or lose young families to other churches in the area. The board of the church was divided. What should they do? After hours of deliberation, the pastor suggested that protecting eighteen month's worth of expenses was unnecessary. The chairman agreed and challenged the board to cash out twelve months' worth of expenses and leave six months' worth in reserves. With some hesitation, the board decided to move forward.

The capital made available in that one decision was enough to make all the necessary renovations without having to ask anyone for a penny in special contributions. When parents brought their babies to the new space, they were overwhelmed with the changes. One of the parents sent the pastor a note thanking the church for investing in her child in such a spectacular way. She told the pastor that she had begun bringing friends who also had young children and needed a church home.

Of course, setting aside money in a reserve fund may be a wise idea, but no one would dare argue that the decision to invest that money in ministry was a bad one. Lives were impacted for eternity as a result of that decision, and it was worth it. Our point in sharing this is simple: we must adopt a new way of thinking about church and the way we handle money. Our perspective must be grounded in a willingness to allow the resources we possess to flow through us in order to change the lives of people around us. Generously pouring out what God has given us to steward, or giving sacrificially even at a time when there doesn't seem to be a surplus, will enable us to connect with people in a lost world and earn us the right to share with them the way home to God.

If we are open to the transformative power of generosity in our own lives, we will become the light and salt, the city on a hill, that Jesus talks about in his Sermon on the Mount. And when the principles of our faith and our financial habits align, we will discover a security that cannot be explained as anything less than supernatural. The security this world offers — through money and possessions — is nothing compared with the eternal security we have in knowing that we belong to God forever, that nothing can separate us from his love for us in Christ. This love frees us from our attachment to the things of this world and gives us a new boldness to serve others.

And it is that supernatural sense of security that will attract the interest of people who do not yet know God. A sense of purpose, meaning, and satisfaction comes when we have a balanced and biblical understanding of the role of money in our lives. Even greater is what happens when members of a church act together in a spirit of generosity to unleash tangible blessings in the lives of people in their community and around the world. There is perhaps no greater evidence of true faith than when our actions match our words.

Generosity, when motivated by a genuine love for God, is contagious, drawing others to wonder why people would give of themselves while expecting nothing in return. In fact, a life — and a church community — that is characterized by generosity may be the most compelling, effective evangelism strategy we have as followers of Christ.

Key Ideas

- Money and its role in our lives provide everyone a common ground and a common experience.
- There is no better time than the present to talk about money.
- An invitation to an unbeliever to participate in an act of generosity may be more spiritually formative than attending your worship service.
- Generosity is the place where the Great Commandment and the Great Commission meet.
- It's possible for people outside the Christian faith to support the ministry of your church; they just need something compelling and to see an impact.
- Hosting a generosity weekend makes a statement that our church is different from what many visitors expect.
- Giving illustrates the rediscovery of the balance between proclaiming the gospel and promoting social justice.
- You cannot fake generosity. It's so attractive that it will eventually cause nonbelievers to notice and ask more questions.

Discussion Questions

1. Have you ever considered generosity to be part of your outreach strategy? Why or why not?
2. What act of generosity could your church perform that would cause people to invite their friends to participate or — at the very least — watch in person?
3. How are you connecting the ministry of your church to the people in your community?
4. In what ways are you creatively thinking about generosity as a way to build bridges to your community and the people who are not part of your church?

CONCLUSION
THERE IS NO GENEROSITY BUTTON

> Every man takes the limits of his own field of vision for the
> limits of the world.   —*Arthur Schopenhauer*

Congratulations, you've just waded through ten of the most significant observations we've made in our careers working with church
leaders and churches. Again, we want to emphasize that our comments in this book do not amount to a step-by-step guide to full
funding for your church. That was never our intention. But we
do hope that some of the ideas we've shared have resonated with
you, have provided a language for you to use when talking with
staff, lay leaders, and your congregation. And have given you some
practical guidance to help you begin this journey with confidence.

Perhaps the greatest risk is that you'll finish reading this book,
add it to your shelf, check it off your list, and never implement any
of the ideas we've discussed. That would be a tragedy indeed! So
now we want to help you transition from the ideas swirling in your
head to real life. We hope this final section of the book will offer
you the ability to move forward with purpose and confidence.

Hoping Is Not a Strategy

Nothing will ever get done, in any area of your life or ministry,
if you never turn your good intentions into concrete actions. You
know how it is. Perhaps you've convinced yourself that you'll start

exercising tomorrow. Or start that Bible reading plan tomorrow. The list can go on and on. People have an uncanny way of putting off till tomorrow what should be started today. Hoping that your church will develop a strong culture of generosity isn't enough. Developing that culture requires regular attention and a deliberate plan. We feel privileged to have invested our careers in helping church leaders do just that. And much of what we do, in addition to providing strategy and perspective, is to provide accountability for the pastors and leaders we serve.

Someone on your staff, or a key volunteer leader, will have to step up and lead in this movement of generosity in your church. Someone has to be the champion. Without a true champion, it will not be a lasting part of your ministry. Pull out your organizational chart or contact list and decide who that person will be. Don't just default that responsibility to the financial person on your staff. Perhaps you're in a position to hire someone for that specific position. If not, then you need to empower someone to hold the entire staff accountable for promoting the principles and precepts of generosity. This of course does not relieve the responsibilities of the senior pastor, who must continue to champion generosity through preaching, teaching about money, and discipling high-capacity givers.

Generosity Is Intentional

At the risk of sounding cliché, being generous requires intentionality. In everything we do as church leaders, we must move with purpose toward our desired result. And to create a culture of generosity, we must resist our natural tendencies to avoid talking about money and learn to speak about it freely and openly. As stated previously, we must begin to normalize the conversation to eliminate unhealthy feelings and viewpoints. As you conduct strategic planning for your church, you should ask yourself whether your plans are moving you toward a more generous culture or farther from it.

When someone in your church is intentionally leading this movement of generosity, that person can ensure that generosity doesn't become just one more item on the church's checklist but instead becomes an important reality that animates everything the church does. Under the leadership of the senior pastor and in partnership with other staff and leaders, this person will have the privilege of helping to create a culture of generosity and giving in your church.

The Cumulative Effect

As we've said, the creation of a culture of generosity is not accomplished in a few easy steps. It is unlikely that some very wealthy giver is just going to walk through your church doors and drop a big check in the offering. That may temporarily solve your church's financial woes, but it won't transform your people, filling their hearts with the Christlike generosity that should be a part of every Christian's life. Changing a culture takes time and constant adjustments. The churches that have been most successful at creating a culture of generosity don't always immediately see the impact of their efforts.

We can't expect to just push a button and make it all happen. It's a process that takes time, and that process isn't something to resent; it's something to embrace. Over time we will learn to do the right things in the right way, and see results in the church and in the lives of our people.

If we are to experience the impact of a culture of generosity, we must recognize that consistent effort and activity is more valuable than a sprint toward the finish line. You didn't grow your church in a day. You didn't come up with the right combination of staff and volunteer leadership in a single planning meeting. And you didn't learn how to communicate a transformational message overnight either. Neither can we expect to create a culture of generosity by reading a book, taking a few notes, and making a few inconsistent attempts at implementing some creative ideas.

It is essential that we constantly make adjustments based on what we're learning and the opportunities that arise. The ability to make decisions and adjustments with clarity and a sense of urgency is key to leading a growing organization and to experiencing the cumulative effect of our efforts.

Generosity and the Big Picture

Perhaps it is the comprehensive nature of generosity that makes pursuing it both exhilarating and daunting at the same time. The call to generosity challenges every part of our individual and corporate lives, leaving no stone unturned, as we grow less attached to this world and more attached to the things of God.

When we, as individuals, begin to understand true generosity, we recognize that it affects not only our giving habits but also every area of our lives. The same is true for churches. We've seen staff realign leadership roles, rewrite job descriptions, rethink plans for spiritual formation and discipleship, and readjust preaching schedules, all in the name of becoming a more generous church. Generosity also reminds us of our own humanity. We are on this earth to worship Christ, share the gospel, and serve others. A generous church understands that none of these things can be accomplished effectively without making generosity one of its core values.

Generosity Is Fundamental to Spiritual Formation

A lot of our time with church leaders is spent discussing and rethinking spiritual formation. It is not uncommon for us to interview the discipleship pastor and his or her team as part of the assessment process. The same is true for the preaching or teaching team. We also spend time working through how a given faith community defines what it means to be a Christ follower. This begins with assimilation, continues with Sunday school, small groups, or missional communities, and is completed with effective preaching and teaching.

One of the most critical things for a church to do well is the task of incorporating new members into the church. Your ability to do this effectively will impact the length of time a member stays in the church and whether that person becomes a vital part of the ministry. If visitors to your church perceive that you consider generosity to be a core value, it will strengthen the culture of generosity in your congregation.

You should have a discipleship plan ready that reinforces the habits of generosity, so that as visitors become regular attenders, you can implement the plan. Church leaders frequently follow a spiritual formation or discipleship plan that outlines certain goals to be achieved over a specific period of time. In a generous church, these goals should include exposing members to what it means to live a generous life: overcoming debt, learning to give, percentage giving, sacrificial giving, estate planning, and the like. If the church doesn't provide the path for a church member's journey of generosity, how can we expect people to know what steps to take?

You can't expect people to develop a genuine heart of generosity if your church addresses the subject only when it launches a capital campaign or faces a financial crisis. A culture of generosity grows when we see generosity throughout all of Scripture, establishing it deep within our church and reinforcing it through discipleship programs. Only then will we witness the powerful result of this new culture: transformed lives.

The Next Steps

What are the most important steps that you can take next to ensure that you maximize the ideas, concepts, and practical tips included in this book? We'd like to offer seven for you to consider.

1. Assemble your staff and/or key leaders and tell them what you've learned from reading this book. Consider reading it together as a group.

2. Assess the current culture of generosity in your church, using the ten observations we have covered in the ten chapters of this book. How would you grade your church? Where are you strong? Where are you weak? What should you start doing? What should you stop doing? What can you change immediately? What can you commit to changing over a period of time?

3. Evaluate your own personal habits related to money and generosity. You never lead people to a place you haven't already been. Look for opportunities to talk about your personal habits, victories, and struggles, and invite others to join you on a new journey toward God-inspired generosity.

4. Set expectations for yourself and your staff in the areas of generosity. Talk openly and graciously with them about giving and stewardship. Remember, we all need encouragement and accountability.

5. Make generosity part of the teaching plan of your church. In everything from small groups to the weekend worship service, commit to talking about money in ways that are consistent with the Bible and God's intention.

6. Commit to preaching a series on generosity as soon as possible (and then regularly thereafter). This will help set the tone and pace for the congregation from the beginning of this effort. Remember that generosity should be a thread that runs through all of our preaching, so don't let this be the only time you talk about money from the pulpit.

7. Plan an act of outrageous generosity in which the entire church can participate. Perhaps you could announce it as part of the new preaching series. Build up to it. You

might plan a special project in the community, arrange to give away one week's worth of offerings, or commit to collecting funds for an international effort. Whatever it is, make it big enough that people will be challenged to dream big and give beyond what they think is their maximum capacity.

These seven steps are just suggestions and are by no means exhaustive, but we hope that they will help jump-start a generosity revolution in your church, a movement that will redefine your understanding of money and ministry. If you will intentionally pursue this challenge of creating a culture of generosity, we can guarantee one thing: you and your church will never be the same.

Where Are You?

Before you leap into a generosity effort in your church, take some time to explore your own feelings about money. Are you preoccupied with money? We spend a lot of time worrying about stuff we have no control over, including the economy. We often waste too much time being anxious about the future—and about the future of our money. As Christ followers, this is no way to live.

Jesus knows about worry. He speaks about it very specifically: "Do not worry about your life, what you will eat or drink; or about your body, what you will wear. Is not life more than food, and the body more than clothes?" (Matt. 6:25). Jesus also says, "No one can serve two masters; for either he will hate the one and love the other, or else he will be loyal to the one and despise the other. You cannot serve God and mammon" (v. 24 NKJV).

When Jesus says, "mammon," he is referring to money in the strongest possible terms: the false god of riches. When riches become an object of devotion, mammon becomes an idol. Meaning it has the power to control our thoughts and our lives like a god.

Jesus knows that this inappropriate preoccupation with money is a serious problem for us, so he prescribes the solution, in effect saying, "Stop worrying; I will take care of you." But to find the strength to stop worrying, we must address a deeper heart issue. We have to stop trying to worship at two altars. We need to get up from the altar we've made to mammon and worship at the one true altar.

As church leaders, we must remember that the people we serve are perceptive. We can't fool them. They will follow what we do more closely than what we say. Is your view of money perpetuating fear and worry, or is it projecting a bold confidence in the providence of God?

Where Is Your Church?

As we mentioned in the seven steps earlier, it's often difficult for leaders to get an accurate picture of the culture of their churches, because their perspective is too narrow. They can't see the issues because they are surrounded by them. Leaders on the front lines of any effort struggle to see the big picture with clarity. That's why it can be helpful to invite in others from the outside. A trusted friend or consultant who understands what it takes to create a culture of generosity can bring a perspective that you lack internally. And it's also important to have a process for receiving feedback from the congregation and ministry staff, who can help you evaluate how far along your church is on the journey toward generosity.

After reading a book like this, many pastors may gather up the staff and key leaders, throw a bunch of good ideas on paper, and try to implement them all at the same time. This sort of shotgun approach never works. It's not about creating a bunch of activity. It is about moving forward with clearly defined goals and expectations.

If inspiring generosity in your church becomes just one more thing to add to your list, you'll never fully realize its potential to radically transform your church's culture. Making it a to-do item to check off diminishes the transformational impact that generosity can have in your personal life and in the life of your church.

The Opportunity Is Yours

As we have said, in the world of nonprofits, the church has what we have called the "home field advantage." Although people are more mobile than ever and many "regular" church attenders come to church only twice a month, the church is the only nonprofit entity that has the opportunity to look its people in the eye fifty-two times a year. This advantage has always been important, but since the global recession began, it has become even more critical for developing generosity. The economic meltdown has reframed the rules for raising the generosity level of the church. Givers are still willing to give, but they are more careful to evaluate the choices they have for their charitable giving. Because of the home field advantage, the church has the opportunity to distinguish itself in a way that invites God's people to invest his resources in the kingdom.

The question for church leaders is, What do I do with this home field advantage? Remember these six things.

1. *Build trust.* All charitable funding is given in an atmosphere of trust. Leverage the weekend worship experience by building trust in all you do.
2. *Cast (and recast) vision.* People have to be constantly reminded of the ministry vision of the church because vision leaks. There are three types of reminders—blast (fire hose), soak (garden hose), drip (soaker hose). There is an appropriate time for each. Use the blast sparingly, and follow with soak and drip to make sure your people absorb the vision.
3. *Shape culture.* You can have great vision, but bad culture trumps good vision every time. Culture is never neutral; it is either for you or against you. Make sure you

are intentionally shaping culture so that you are calling your people to live generously.

4. *Demonstrate impact.* More than ever before, because of the recession that started in 2008, givers are carefully evaluating the choices for their charitable investments. Impact is like the ministry return on investment, or mROI. Where givers see it, they direct their charitable giving. You probably have stories of impact in your ministry, but they may be hidden in the numbers. Make sure you communicate both the numbers and the stories.

5. *Enhance relationships.* People give to people. Build relationships with the people in your church and community who can fund the mission.

6. *Highlight good stewardship.* Churches that practice good stewardship with the money given to them earn givers' respect. Let your people know about key decisions you make to more efficiently use the funds entrusted to your church.

Check your church against this list. Which of these things are you doing? Which are you not doing? Don't ignore the home field advantage.

Generosity Changes Everything

We have seen firsthand that people who embrace a lifestyle of generosity experience abundance. Pastors who guide ministry staff and other leaders along the journey toward generosity experience abundance. Churches that embrace generosity as a core value experience abundance. It is no accident that all who experience abundance must first mature in generosity.

Though this may seem paradoxical, to us it makes perfect sense. Time and time again, we've seen that people who work so hard to protect and preserve all they have end up losing it. And those who freely give from the resources they never claimed to own end up gaining more.

Generosity is a paradox, in that we gain by giving. But paradox is a common feature of our faith: Jesus gave his life that we might gain life forever; a person who saves his life will lose it, while someone who loses his life for Christ's sake will find it; and the first will be last, but the last will be first. So it's no surprise that the paradox holds for our spirit of generosity.

We believe that Christ followers who are pursuing generous lives provide the clearest picture of God to others. The church is God's plan to carry forward the gospel until Christ returns and all things are made new. In the meantime, we have been given the opportunity to take our stories, our faith, and our resources and share them with others. Our willingness to do this without restraint speaks volumes about the extent to which we've embraced and been changed by the gospel.

There is no room for anything less than abundance in living and generosity in giving, for we serve a God who has abundant resources and has already provided the greatest example of generosity this world has ever known.

Simply put, generosity changes everything.

ACKNOWLEDGMENTS

We are each deeply grateful for the leadership of our pastors, Randy Pope of Perimeter Church in Atlanta and David Loveless of Discovery Church in Orlando. Their desire to model generosity to their congregations has been an inspiration to us.

We also want to acknowledge our colleagues at Leadership Network and Generis. Simply put, they are among the most committed and effective people on the planet, and it is a privilege, not to mention lots of fun, to serve alongside them. Our iron is sharper because of them.

And last, but not least, we want to thank the pastors and leaders of the churches we have had the privilege to coach over the years along this journey of generosity. What we know about generosity has come from observing you as you have stepped out in faith to lead your people. We honor you as we put what we have learned into writing.

Leadership Network Innovation Series

Real Stories.
Innovative Ideas.
Transferable
Truths.

How can you fulfill your calling as a ministry leader and help your church experience vitality? Learn from those who have gone before you.

The Leadership Network Innovation Series presents case studies and insights from leading practitioners and pioneering churches that are successfully navigating the ever-changing streams of spiritual renewal in modern society. Each book offers *real* stories about *real* leaders in *real* churches doing *real* ministry.

The Big Idea
Dave Ferguson, Jon Ferguson & Eric Bramlett

Bridges to Grace
Liz Swanson & Teresa McBean

Confessions of a Reformission Rev.
Mark Driscoll

Contagious Generosity
Chris Willard & Jim Sheppard

Dangerous Church
John Bishop

Deliberate Simplicity
Dave Browning

Ethnic Blends
Mark DeYmaz & Harry Li

Insourcing: Bringing Discipleship Back to the Local Church
Randy Pope

Leadership from the Inside Out
Kevin Harney

Love without Walls
Laurie Beshore

The Monkey and the Fish
Dave Gibbons

The Multi-Site Church Revolution
Geoff Surratt, Greg Ligon & Warren Bird

A Multi-Site Church Roadtrip
Geoff Surratt, Greg Ligon & Warren Bird

Servolution
Dino Rizzo

Sticky Church
Larry Osborne

The Surge
Pete Briscoe with Todd Hillard

Learn more at www.InnovationSeries.net

About Leadership Network

Since 1984, Leadership Network has fostered church innovation and growth by diligently pursuing its far-reaching mission statement: *To identify high-capacity Christian leaders, to connect them with other leaders, and to help them multiply their impact.*

While specific techniques may vary as the church faces new opportunities and challenges, Leadership Network consistently focuses on bringing together entrepreneurial leaders who are pursuing similar ministry initiatives. The resulting peer-to-peer interaction, dialogue, and collaboration—often across denominational lines—helps these leaders better refine their individual strategies and accelerate their own innovations.

To further enhance this process, Leadership Network develops and distributes highly targeted ministry tools and resources, including books, DVDs and videotapes, special reports, e-publications, and free downloads.

For additional information on the mission or activities of Leadership Network, please contact:

Leadership ✕ Network
Innovation Series
800-765-5323
www.leadnet.org
client.care@leadnet.org